ETHICS

IN THE SERVICE OF THE SICK

Charles G. Vella

ETHICS

IN THE SERVICE OF THE SICK

Reflections and Experiences of Life
at the San Raffaele Hospital, Milan

With Foreword by Dermod McCarthy

VERITAS

First published by Edizioni Paoline, Milano, 2007
This edition published in 2009 by
Veritas Publications
7/8 Lower Abbey Street
Dublin I
Ireland
Email publications@veritas.ie
Website www.veritas.ie

ISBN 978 I 84730 I66 6

10 9 8 7 6 5 4 3 2 I

A catalogue record for this book is available from the British Library.

Translated by Brigid Garroni and Georgette Booker
Designed by Barbara Croatto
Printed in the Republic of Ireland by ColourBooks Ltd., Dublin

Veritas books are printed on paper made from the wood pulp of managed forests. For
every tree felled, at least one tree is planted, thereby renewing natural resources.

'No riches can outweigh bodily health,
no enjoyment surpass a cheerful heart.'

(Ecclesiasticus 30:16)

For all the doctors
and the nurses
at the San Raffaele Hospital,
and especially for the dear patients
who have taught me so much about life.

CONTENTS

FOREWORD

Two friends and neighbours travelled to Dublin to visit a terminally ill farmer from Tipperary, a county famed throughout Ireland for the prowess of its hurling team. After giving him the local news, they assured him that he would regain full health within a few months and be with them the following summer to celebrate Tipperary thrashing Cork in the Munster Hurling Final. The patient nodded and the visitors left. A young, newly appointed chaplain to the hospital overheard the final exchange and approached the bedside when the others had gone. The patient murmured, 'I suppose they had to say that, Father. I hope they feel better now! You know and they know that I won't see any more hurling games.'

That little scene encapsulates the unreality, the pretence that often surrounds our relationship with the seriously ill. The image of that resigned nod has never faded from my memory, for I was the young chaplain recently assigned to St Anne's Cancer Hospital in Dublin. There were many lessons to be learned in the 'classroom of the bedside' in St Anne's. How I wish I had had a book like this one by Charles Vella as my *vade mecum* then!

As Fr Vella found when sent to visit a young woman who was near death in Chicago, I too was often confronted by the woeful inadequacy of my preparation for working in a chaplaincy role with sick people, with their families and carers. The training we received as student priests for dealing with the ill was limited to the rubrics of administering the sacrament of Extreme Unction. Thankfully, welcome advances have been made since then in the formation and training of pastoral care professionals in our hospitals and nursing homes.

As national health services become ever more bureaucratic and the notion of a vocation to healing sinks under the weight of economic imperatives, there is all the more reason to recall the Judaeo-Christian vision of the child of God in each patient. Fr Vella echoes James Schall SJ: 'the essence of civilization, ethics and dignity (of man) is that all life ... deserves to be lived'.

To be lived! Charles Vella, in his own life story, embodies the words of Christ: 'I have come so that they may have life and have it to the full' (Jn 10: 10). My first encounter with this dynamic Maltese priest happened in Dar-es-Salaam in 1974 at an international congress on the family organised jointly by the Christian Family Movement and the World Council of Churches. Fr Vella was the driving force behind the two-week event which drew couples in their hundreds from many Christian denominations and all parts of the globe. The objectives were two-fold: to highlight before the world the importance of the family in society, and to gain insights from the community and family values underlying the political theory then in practice in Tanzania under the inspired leadership of President Julius Nyerere.

My involvement was in producing a television documentary on this unique congress, subsequently broadcast in various countries. It was Charles Vella who invited us to come to Dar, to film the proceedings, interview the experts, and bring the message of the essential role of the family unit to a wider audience.

It was this deep concern for the recognition and well-being of families around the world that led to his long association with the sick, with the San Raffaele Hospital in Milan as his base. But Fr Vella is not a man to confine his work to one particular medical institution. Through his membership of European healthcare committees and his contributions to a variety of medical and ethical journals, he has become a respected advocate of a holistic approach to healthcare. For him, a sick man or woman is not just the patient in bed number twelve, or 'the kidney' in the end cubicle, but a person made in the image and likeness of God, deserving of not only the best medical attention, but the care and love of a family and community.

This book, the fruit of Fr Vella's ministry at personal, national and international levels, will provide valuable insights not only for professional healthcare workers, but for all who are in contact with the sick, either at home or in hospital. Its narrative style removes it from the realm of weighty academic study and makes the riches within accessible to all. Read, learn and enjoy!

DERMOD MCCARTHY
Former Editor of Religious Programmes RTÉ
Pastoral Care Facilitator RTÉ
February 2009

INTRODUCTION

This book sets out to give a humane face to ethics, that of the patient both as a person and as an image and likeness of God – *imago Dei*.

These pages have grown out of my experiences at the bedside of patients – what is called 'bedside ethics'; they are reflections on the many ethical questions posed by patients, doctors and nurses, particularly those which have come up over my twenty years of service within the San Raffaele Hospital in Milan, which I have always loved and will continue to love.

Since the founding of the Cana Movement in Malta in 1954 for the preparation of couples for marriage, pastoral work with and counselling of families, I have continued to work closely with families in various countries. My interest in this area brought me to Italy, at the invitation of the Commission for the Family of the Italian Bishops' Conference, at that time presided over by the late bishop Monsignor Pietro Fiorelli di Prato.

I have been greatly inspired and helped in my mission by Carl Rogers, the noted humanist-existentialist American psychologist, one of the first to expound the concept of 'person-centred therapy', which to me meant that putting the well-being and the rights of a patient and his or her family before every other consideration is imperative.[1]

In these pages I have attempted to give everyday ethics a humane face using a narrative style which I hope is not only easily comprehensible but also stimulating.

On the other hand, in expounding ethical principles and facts, I hope to encourage and stimulate not only a critical conscience aimed at denouncing the many negative practices which ought to be banished from the treatment of patients, but also a new prospect of life open to hope.

Making recourse to biblical, theological and magisterial references, I hope to throw light on the holistic treatment and care of the sick in order that the 'helping relationship' (Rogers) may be in accordance with the evangelical logic of receiving with compassion, of 'giving', of caring for others.

It is no coincidence that this work is centred on the realities of the San Raffaele, Scientific University Institute of Treatment and Research, since it is in this 'temple of medicine and suffering' that I have exercised my ministry of management, always in the role of 'priestly-doctor'. This by no means suggests that the San Raffaele is an ethical oasis, or that it is the only hospital which treats patients humanely, for the humanisation of medical care is nowadays widespread. I simply wish to emphasise that I was called to the San Raffaele to 'teach and heal' by Providence. It was from the San Raffaele Foundation's philosophy that I learned that 'each patient is, before all else, a human being' and that every sick person is *Jesus, Deus Patiens* (Christ, the suffering God).

With all my heart I thank all who work at the San Raffaele, from its president down to the workers, for all the benefit I have received through my long years of experience here which now gives me the grace of being able to cast the net wide.

I also wish to thank Brigid Garrone for her professional help, Richard Muscat, former Maltese Ambassador to Ireland, and my long-time friend, Dermod McCarthy, for writing the foreword to this book (which puts me in mind of my many other Irish friends: Jo Dunne, Des Forrestal, William Fitzgerald, Eamon Casey and a host of others). I thank you all.

CHARLES G. VELLA

NOTE

1   C.G. Vella, *Caring: The Family and the Patient, an Interdisciplinary Approach*, ed. V.A. Ferrari, Ferrari Publishing, Bergamo, 2003.

CHAPTER 1

WHEN THE PATIENT IS A NUMBER

To introduce our subject, I shall quote a letter to the editor of the *Corriere della Sera*, which featured as the 'Story of the Day' on 24 June 2005 and elicited a response from Giangiacomo Schiavi, a regular columnist with the paper. Increasingly, the printed media and TV give space to the publication of the negative experiences and the disillusionment caused by the poor quality of care given in hospitals and clinics to members of the public. The writer of this letter, therefore, is not a voice in the wilderness, but I shall quote it in its entirety because it indicates a 'typical' example of the malfunction of the health services. The Italian word is 'malasanità', a word which has entered the Italian language in daily use, even if it is sometimes misused.

The title, spread over five columns of print, screamed: HOSPITALS: WHEN THE PATIENT IS MERELY A NUMBER. This is what the letter said:

> I went to a hospital in Milan to care for my ailing father and found the attitude of doctors and nurses to be cold and distant. What really struck me was the psychological degradation of the sick. It was like going back in time to the immediate post-war period, where, like lottery numbers, patients were identified and called by the numbers assigned to their beds. Doctors and nurses would come in and call out: 'Who's number 12?'
>
> A few days later my father was brutally given the cold facts about his condition with no thought to the psychological effects of such bad news. This does not foster good doctor-patient relations. Is it not a fact that medical treatments have a greater chance of success when the patient is willing to collaborate with his carers?

The letter speaks for itself, and Schiavi replied to it in a very correct and humane manner. When patients become mere numbers, something is missing from the bedside manner of carers: it is a sense of ethics, the lack of which is to blame for the so-called 'malfunction' of the health services. If a patient becomes a number it is because a certain deep sensitivity is missing in the attitude of care-givers, which results in a malfunctioning of inter-personal relationships.

Hospital wards are not populated by numbers, but by men and women of different ages, nationalities and creeds, who have been hospitalised because they are ill. Very often, their suffering is augmented by the humiliation of being thought of as a number on a bed, totally divested of their human dignity: they become mere objects, and are often treated as such, without consideration or courtesy.

The greatest humiliation for patients is that, being thought of as a number, they are deprived of their dignity. Nobody should be treated in such a way. All individuals have the right of respect to their human dignity, whether they are patients in a luxurious private hospital or in a public ward. Even more degrading is the inhumane treatment of psychiatric patients by certain members of staff in mental institutions, as has been amply shown in a number of appalling cases. The same holds for aged members of society who are not self-sufficient, are incontinent or unable to feed themselves, who throw tantrums and shout or cry loudly in their rage and frustration. God loves every person, but these are his favourite children: why then do not those who work among them have the least spark of love, compassion or respect for their vulnerable brethren?

As was stated in Schiavi's reply to the published letter, it used to be common, in the past, to hear doctors, nurses and other hospital staff call out instructions of the type: 'An intravenous drip for number 8; a lozenge for number 17', as though calling out 'numbers' in a bingo hall. Added to this, 'each of these "numbers" were subjected to being addressed in an overly familiar manner to which they had no choice but submit, whether they were asking for information about their condition or attempting to safeguard their dignity.'[1]

Merely the necessity of having to undergo a stay in hospital is traumatic enough for patients, especially those suffering serious illness. I have witnessed the fear, uncertainty and doubt of patients of all ages being admitted into hospital, both before and during my ministry at the San Raffaele. They are often psychologically at rock bottom, as may be seen by the pallor of their faces, and at times, the odd tear. Being referred to by number on their arrival in the ward adds to their suffering.

I remember once accompanying a woman to a luxury clinic where she was received in a very professional manner, but on finding herself alone in her hotel-like room, she felt that she had just been shut into a fridge. Even though she was not assigned a number and was always addressed as 'Madam', the atmosphere of the place was cold and unwelcoming. It is not the papered walls nor the aesthetically pleasing building and furnishings that constitute a hospital worthy of the name, it is the people who work there: the head of surgery, the nurses, the nursing aides and so on down to the domestics. These may create a welcoming atmosphere which puts patients at their ease, calms them down and fosters their trust.

It is human warmth towards the patient which renders a tangible ethical sense in human relations. In my experience, and doubtlessly that of many patients, there are many doctors and other health workers whose attitudes show a real ethical conscience.

As a matter of fact, as a priest myself, I have observed that there is a sizeable number of 'good samaritans' within the ranks of the health services, who are dedicated to their profession in the same way as a priest lives his vocation. I remember an elderly military gentleman who walked through the hospital ward proudly wearing his war medals and telling anyone who would listen the stories of how he had won each of them. He was never called 'Number 20' but always 'The General' and this made him happy. To him, the hospital was home and the staff were his friends. For months towards the end of his life he battled the illness that afflicted him, and to the very end he was referred to and addressed as 'The General'. He died like a true general.

PERSON-CENTRED HEALTHCARE

The well-known human existentialist psychologist Carl Rogers was among the first to develop the concept of 'person-centred therapy', which involves the ethical imperative of giving priority to the 'well-being' and the 'good' of every person, sick or healthy, without discrimination. The individual is of absolute value, and must be considered objectively in his totality and unity a creature of God, made 'in his image and likeness'. Treatment and cure must therefore be holistic, that is, caring for the person in both body and spirit.

All hospital and medical staff, including administrative staff, must always act in the best interests of the patient. Unhappily there are times when budgetary exigencies make profits and expenses more important to the 'hospital industry' (a most unfortunate term) than the well-being of each patient.

According to Professor Edmond Pellegrino, who for many years directed the Kennedy Institute for Ethics at Georgetown University in Washington DC, the term 'medical good' refers both to the effects of medical procedure on the illness that is being treated and to the benefits that may be achieved by the application of medical knowledge: prevention, cure, quality of and prolongation of life. The 'medical benefits' can vary. For example, the use of an oxygen mask may lead to a complete recovery, but it can also cause a patient to have a panic attack; for such reasons it is necessary to weigh the pros and cons of any treatment. Pellegrino notes that the usual procedure is to weigh the medical benefits against the effect on the individual patient and act accordingly.

Values such as freedom, rights, rationality, awareness, the right to take decisions regarding treatment and the ability to choose are associated with the well-being of the patient. When patients are thought of as numbers, their well-being is relegated to second place, because the ethic of human-centred medical treatment is missing.

In this day and age, the human person and human life are considered of little worth – this is evident if one notices the ease with which people are murdered, wars are declared. As stated in Pope John Paul II's encyclical *Dominum et vivificantem*: 'Despite the dizzyingly rapid technoscientific progress, despite the great achievements and the goals reached, mankind is threatened, humanity is threatened.'[2] In this same document the Pope writes about the 'picture of death' and the 'culture of death' which is being composed in our times.[3]

To change this it is necessary to make a great improvement in the treatment and care of the sick, putting them first, making them protagonists – far from treating them as anonymous numbers – in hospitals worthy of human beings, thus rendering their confinement in hospital a humane experience. Such change involves a revolution in health policy and hospital management: it necessitates viewing the patient as a citizen with full rights, deserving of respect because he or she is a person who is suffering and should be treated, no matter the cost.

In some countries, as in Great Britain, where the health service has been partially privatised, hospitals sometimes refuse treatment or surgical procedure, even those as necessary as organ transplants, because their budget cannot cope with the expenses involved. One such example involved a girl who was refused treatment by a number of hospitals that lacked the funds to cover the costs, and was eventually allowed into a hospital and given treatment when an anonymous benefactor offered to make good for all the expense needed. This is a classical example of utilitarian ethics, in which the cost of treatment is considered more important than the needs of the patient.

Rogers' philosophy on the human person is not ascetic, neutral, political or beaurocratic, but is based on human and moral values whereby the individual person is 'the agent' and 'protagonist'.

THE LONG WAITING TIMES FOR ADMISSION INTO HOSPITAL

What deeply dehumanises the patient-doctor relationship is the long time one must wait before being admitted into hospital or being operated on. This is a common reality in many EU countries; unfortunately Italy holds the record for longest waiting times. According to the Active Citizenship Network (European Active Citizenship Network – Patients' Tribunal), in the majority of cases the waiting lists in Italy are longer than those in nine other European countries. This causes psychological distress to patients and undermines their quality of life.

This situation exists in other countries, but the waiting times are shorter, with a few exceptions. When the wait is too long, the patient is often forced to make an appointment with a hospital that has comparatively shorter waiting lists, for example one in the north of Italy rather than in the south, or even in different countries altogether, where some procedures are carried out using more modern methods. I know many patients who have done this, among them some doctors: for hip replacements one travels to the UK; for liver transplants to Berlin or Brussels; for knee operations to Lyons; for neurosurgery to Innsbruck; and for oncological treatment to Paris. There have been a number of court rulings confirming the right of European citizens to be treated in European countries other than their own; and the European Court of Justice has ruled that patients should be reimbursed for treatment, travelling and lodging expenses in cases where waiting lists in their country of origin were judged to be too long.

It is unacceptable that, as often happens, hospitals should suggest that patients seek expensive private treatment in order to avoid a long wait. Such a proposal may be acceptable to patients covered by medical insurance, but is not practicable for the vast majority, many of whom often require urgent treatment but are forced to wait months, to the detriment of their health which may consequently deteriorate beyond a state where their condition is curable. This goes against all ethical principles and denies the citizen the right to benefit from public health services within a reasonable time frame.

Since April 2004 mutual healthcare cooperation agreements between EU countries gives EU citizens the right to free treatment anywhere within the EU, but this only holds true in cases where highly specialised treatment is unavailable in Italy, or specific treatments are unavailable at the time they are needed, or are available but unsuited to the specific needs of particular patients. It is then also necessary to acquire the endorsement of the regional authority for such treatment.

On the other hand, it must be stated that health welfare regulations are generous with the over-65s, low-income families, the unemployed, the chronically ill and children under the age of six, while millions of Italians are exempt from prescription or other medical charges. It has been calculated that there are between 22 and 23 million Italians (40 per cent) who do not pay for visits to a specialist, analysis and diagnosis of illnesses. This number is further raised to 34 million by those entitled to free medicinals.[4] Only eight regions are left where patients must pay a 'ticket' (€10 to €20) for medical services or medicinals.

This situation leaves much to be desired from the point of view of justice, equality and honesty. It is necessary to move on, as other countries have done, from a welfare state to a caring society; that is, a society that is not satisfied with a state that acts as parent.

THE REALITY OF THE HEALTH SERVICE

The above negative aspects are often characteristic of health services administration. If you go to the local health clinic to get a form filled in by the doctor on duty entitling you to medical examination or analysis, you wait your turn for some hours, despite being sixth in the queue. Then you go to a hospital to make an appointment for the examination, and if you make sure to arrive early in the morning, you will find that you are tenth in line. The receptionist or clerk behind the little window treats you very impersonally. After some days, if you are lucky and line up at 7 a.m., you are twentieth in the queue.

The situation becomes worse when, having been entered into the computerised system as a number, the patient is made to wait for a number of months before being admitted into hospital or being operated upon. In such a situation, the sound of the phone ringing raises the hopes of the patient that this will be a call from the hospital. It takes the intervention of the heavenly saints to be admitted into hospital or be given an ultrasound scan or x-ray in a short time. Some patients die before their turn to be operated on comes around.

White Coats and Pyjamas: The Doctors' Part in the Italian Health Services Disaster by Dr Paolo Cornaglia Ferraris provoked lively and contrasting reactions, bringing about confrontation between doctors and patients. In a second book, entitled *Pyjamas and White Coats: Changes in the Italian Health Services*, the author analyses in a more systematic way the changes taking place in the Italian health services since Minister Bindi's reforms. Treating the sick is defined as 'a dignified and noble profession', and a number of practical proposals are put forward, which aim at humanising medical practice. In order to ensure that patients 'no longer continue to be treated as objects, but are seen as equal stakeholders in their own recovery' the author insists on the need to 'take into account the patient's background and life in the devising of the treatment programme' and insists that one 'should never arrogate to oneself the right to make choices which may be contrary to the wishes of the patient'. This means building a relationship of trust which allows the patient to come to an informed consent in his/her treatment, in other words to share in the choices made by the doctor.[5]

Fortunately there are hospitals in Italy which have gone way beyond this advice in the way patients are treated. Thanks to new technology, the professionalism of the doctors and the support of administrators, many problems of hospital management have been resolved and the patient today is no longer merely a number, but a person who enjoys a citizen's rights to a health service based on an ethic of justice, equality and transparency.

All hospital workers are called to give of their very best to the sick person: one should never bear an attitude of charity or pity towards the sick, but has 'an obligation to provide the most humane, scientifically correct surroundings in the same way as one would provide a golden tabernacle for Christ'.[6]

NOTES

1 Giangiacomo Schiavi, response to a letter by Eleonora Bassi in the *Corriere della Sera*, p. 55.
2 John Paul II, *Dominum et vivificantem*, 65, Vatican Library Editing House, Vatican City 1986.
3 Ibid., 75.
4 Roberto Turno, in *Il Sole 24 ore*, 19 September 2006.
5 P. Cornaglia Ferraris, Laterza, Bari, *Pyjamas and White Coats: Changes in the Italian Health Service*, 2000, pp. 148–9.
6 Principles of the San Raffaele Hospital in Milan.

CHAPTER 2

A young GP in a mountain village once said to his mentor, 'Professor, I've discovered a new medicine'. The professor was perplexed by such an audacious assertion from a former student of his, and asked, 'What is this new medicine?' With a gentle smile the young doctor gave the startling reply: 'Holding my patients' hands and smiling at them while giving my prescription.' St Padre Pio had instructed the doctors at the Casa di Sollievo (Home of Relief) to 'Give a smile with your medicines'. A smile costs nothing to him who gives it, but is worth a great deal to the patient.

This is what humanising medical practice means, treating the patient like a 'brother' or, as one says nowadays, a 'partner' (R. Vitch).

Many hospitals today lack the human touch and medical practice is dehumanising. The buildings are old and patients are crowded into wards, or worse still, lined up in corridors, exposed not only to draughts, but also to the curious looks of passers-by. It is wrong to leave a patient waiting for hours on a gurney in some corridor until an orderly can come and ferry him or her from one section of the hospital to another in order to have tests made. In such cases, patients are likely to contract bronchial pneumonia or some other infection. I have always felt extremely guilty about old patients treated like objects in this way when they have asked me, with tears in their eyes, to call somebody to take them to the bathroom.

Even hospitals boasting the most sophisticated technology cannot be termed institutions of 'excellence' if they lack respect for the human person. We should not make fabulous assumptions about technology, no matter that it enables the patient to travel to the other side of the world to undergo robot-assisted surgery — it does not magic away all problems.

MISTAKES IN MEDICINE

One often reads tragic news reports about medical errors causing inexplicable deaths after, say, an appendectomy, a birth or an operation. Such stories cause anger, but after the footage is shown on TV and the photos have appeared in the papers, it is often all forgotten. At times tribunals for the defence of patients' rights instigate the opening of investigations, but the files are soon archived. Individual doctors may at times be made to bear the brunt of the public's condemnation even when investigations do not turn up any evidence of negligence or unprofessional practices on their part.

In the United States such cases are dealt with by litigation lawyers, who are often to be found hanging around outside hospitals in the hope of nabbing the defence cases of patients who have had unfortunate experiences there. Such events as the birth of a disabled baby, or surgical errors like operating on a healthy eye instead of the one needing treatment, or amputating the wrong leg, are awarded extremely high damages by tribunals. Frequently, the doctors involved in such cases lose their professional warrant and have to fork out millions of euros through insurance agencies.

Keeping in mind that being human we are also fallible, it must be reaffirmed that for the good of all, abuses or errors during medical treatment must be reported without reservation, and the reports need to be backed up by the tribunal which protects the rights of the sick; otherwise there is the danger that the negligence be repeated, against all principles of ethical responsibility towards patients, and affect other patients.

I feel saddened by the way people, especially the old, are left to die alone in hospitals today, and impelled by the testimony of student nurses working in hospital wards on the way things are managed around hospital deathbeds, I proposed that an ethical committee study the issue. Cardinal Carlo Maria Martini, at that time archbishop of Milan, denounced the situation at the Milano Medicina Congress of 1985 with these words: 'Ethics and solidarity have been subordinated to the fees charged by medical practitioners in all fields of medical care; have succumbed to shoddy hospital care, bureaucratisation and the shedding of responsibility on the part of the health care system.' I would answer any question about the way people die in hospital by speaking generally of how the patient on his deathbed is accompanied.[1] For now I shall merely say that in some, even excellent, set-ups, people die alone, without the comfort of their nearest and dearest; in others however, as the Blessed Mother Teresa of Calcutta used to say about her 'poorest of the poor' in the 'Home for the Dying', they 'have lived like animals, now they can die like angels'.

THE SCANDAL OF THE GOOD SAMARITAN

The above statements dishonour a society that is often nowadays termed a 'caring society' in which the individual is supposedly looked after. The truth is that, centuries after Christ told the parable of the Good Samaritan as a way of teaching us how to look after our neighbour, we still feel the need to talk about humanisation. Cardinal Fiorenzo Angelini, who for many years was responsible for pastoral care in the hospitals of Rome and for the Pontifical Council on Health, was right to call this a 'scandalous' fact.

Although this malady has put down roots in the mentality of hospital workers, resulting in their behaving unprofessionally, humanisation is often rare even for the reason that hospitals have become centres of power because of still existing political divisions, interference and factions, budgetary cutbacks and lack of maintenance.

As Weber states, it all boils down to political power and self-interest, and, in privately run hospitals, to the profits of the directors and shareholders. This is all at the expense of the less fortunate: the sick; the handicapped; drug addicts; the disadvantaged.

Politicians tussle for the top positions in the health ministry, whether at government, regional or local levels. They are in charge, and behave in character, often acting in the interests of those who work in their favour rather than in the general interest of all – the citizens who have elected them. This is very serious, for these people's careers are advanced and they are placed in managerial positions for which they are unfit, making mediocre leaders. Mediocrity in public office, as well as in hospitals, suffocates and kills professionalism. Power is entrusted to people who often lack leadership qualities, creativity, management skills or the courage to express their thoughts frankly. They are true 'servants' of those who place them in such positions. This takes place at all levels and is true of some doctors, hospital administrators and other workers. The result is, sadly, a lack of professionalism and transparency.

'If there is a true master in a hospital,' said one African bishop to a community of St John of God, 'it should be the patient.' If only things were always so! Nowadays the decision-makers are financial interest, marketing, the book balance and business. Clinics and old people's homes give good returns, especially if they are backed by regional authorities or government politicians.

Banks do nothing to help humanise hospitals since their financial interests condition hospital management. One of the worst consequences of this situation is the side-lining of administrators who are expert financiers but also honest people, who attempt to introduce measures which are unwelcome to the board of directors. Once these honest and upright people, some of them men and women of faith, are lost, it is hard to have the ethical principles of humanisation approved at board meetings, since most board members focus on finances rather than on the patient.

This is what is happening, or what has already happened, in some truly beautiful clinics which perhaps have been managed in too 'religious' a manner. In one such case, a known financial wizard was brought in to help. Being 'compassionate' of the financial plight of the community of sisters running the clinic, he immediately bought them out, in partnership with an investment company – of course, he did so at a price well below the market value. Poor sisters, they had thought to have found a saviour in this businessman!

A FAILED PROJECT

This situation prompted Cardinal Carlo Maria Martini and some collaborators to summon together a group of around forty religious at the Curia in order to put a stop to such events. Cardinal Martini envisioned the setting up of a federation of hospitals and clinics which, while retaining their autonomy, would collaborate with and help each other using a system of exchanging and sharing sophisticated hospital equipment, thus also sharing out the cost of acquiring such equipment and safeguarding the financial strength of about forty health facilities in Lombardy.

All present listened attentively to Cardinal Martini as he expounded this idea, and at first it was greeted enthusiastically, and the strategic plan was entrusted to a priest who was an expert in the field, being the president of an excellent institution in Milan. However, the project never took off and the Cardinal, whose vision for the future had been to 'throw wide the nets', was extremely disappointed. It had seemed that the idea had been unanimously welcomed, but unfortunately it is difficult for even religious to see eye to eye.

After that, the jackals will come, and the Church, by its sins of omission, allows its healing charism to pass completely into the hands of business and the banks. This will, of course, lead to a complete reorganisation, and the statues of the Madonna of Lourdes and Padre Pio will not be the only things disappearing from the corridors: the humanising environment will also disappear. Hospitals and clinics will seem luxurious places offering hotel-like facilities and service, but people will have to fork out a great deal of money to be admitted there.

The newly built San Raffaele in Rome, a jewel of a hospital and a 'temple of healing', is one such typical example. It is scandalous that this was allowed to happen with only some token questions asked in parliament which were ambiguously answered by the Catholic Minister of Health of the time. It became merely a game of power and lucre, with no thought to the fact that Rome would have been able to have an excellent centre of medical and scientific learning and research on the internationally tried and tested model of the San Raffaele in Milan.

Don Luigi Maria Verzè, the ideator and promoter of the Rome San Raffaele tells this story in his book *A Life for a Life*.[2] He and all other Raffaellians still carry the emotional scars of this event, because the vision of giving a humane and humanising hospital to the Vatican City, whose motto would have been *Jesus, Deus Patiens* (Jesus, the suffering God) in a 'temple of healing', may have been ambitious, but could have been totally realisable for the good of the whole community.

MONSIGNOR GIUSSANI AND THE SAN RAFFAELE

Despite being, like all human creations, imperfect, the San Raffaele attempts, by the efforts of its 4,000 strong workforce, every day to reach perfection. As Monsignor Luigi Giussani, founder of the world-wide Communion and Liberation Movement, often said to me during his long stays in hospital under the care of Dr Melogli and other practitioners: 'Fr Vella, I am sure that the San Raffaele is the work of God and the product of faith.' I am in total agreement with him and believe that the San Raffaele will forever remain a humane, scientific teaching hospital because 'healing is a sacred ministry' and 'no scientific and medical assistance investment can be greater than the value with which God endows human life'.[3]

I hope that this work of God stays always faithful to its original inspiration and genesis, which is to create a hospital for the care and healing of the sick as well as for research purposes, with the aim of humanely improving quality of life, because 'sickness and death are respectively not fatal or invincible: God did not create death', as we read in the Book of Wisdom. 'He made all things that they may live. He made the things born of this world as instruments of health. In them resides no deathly poison.' Don Verzè (pioneer of the University Hospital Research Institute in Milan) usually adds that if there is 'poison' it may be neutralised by the research, to which 400 scientists dedicate their time in the three Department of Biotechnology buildings.

I have used the San Raffaele as an example of a humanised hospital; however, it does not stand alone. There are many other hospitals in Italy with the same history, vision and mission, both government-funded and privately owned.

THE ETHICAL CONSCIENCE

Comfort and aesthetics do not suffice to make a hospital humane and humanising; what is needed is the promotion of a humanistic culture. It is only through the teaching of the art and ethics of medical practice that it is possible to foster a new mentality where the human being is placed at the centre of medical care and research. The fact that the San Raffaele has always taught and acted on the basis of the four solid pillars of treatment and care, research, teaching (by the setting up of the Life-Health University) and management, has always been its winning card. While these four facets of San Raffaele's activity are related and interdependent, teaching, through the permanent formation of socio-medical-health behaviour, is the diamond point at which these four facets come together. It is not nowadays possible to practise holistic medicine without first creating the cultural 'humus' into which philosophical and ethical principles may put down roots. The formation of men and women who work in the health services must take place through programmes encompassing socio-psychological and ethical healthcare. Only by such means may a person-based ethic, which is fundamental to the humanisation of hospitals, take root in doctor-patient, nurse-patient and administrator-patient relations.

John Paul II had promoted an appeal for 'the creation of an ethical conscience'. It is obvious that the individual responsible conscience is formed by the culture and principles of the institution within which that individual works. For this reason an educational process concerning the human person, his rights, interpersonal relationships, human and spiritual values, which together form the humanistic corpus of a hospital, is necessary.

Moreover, it is necessary that this culture of virtue-based ethics[4] be nurtured in future generations of doctors and nurses during their formative years of study. If, as often happens, this aspect of care is lacking, the 'ethical conscience' which leads to the humanisation of hospitals will be missing. Foreign Catholic universities like the Georgetown University in Washington DC, by means of the well-known Kennedy Institute, or Lutheran hospitals through the Park Ridge Centre for Medicine and Religion, in Chicago, hold obligatory courses in 'ethics and humanistic studies'. This is not so in Italy. Despite this fact however, some institutions, like the Gemelli Clinic in Rome, impart a serious and adequate formation to students, which is inspired by Christian values.

THE ETHICS OF THE VIRTUES

Humanisation is lived, witnessed and realised by means of the values instilled in the workers, who should unconditionally accept the founding principles of the hospital in which they work. 'The hospital should be an instrument of personal and professional realisation of the sacredness of the art of healing for its workers even before it is so for its patients.'[5] The worker spends a great part of his or her day in the hospital, grows with the hospital and aspires to achieve job satisfaction in order to realise his/herself as a person. Medicine is a sacred art, to the extent that nowadays one talks of the 'medical priesthood'. However, such a vision of medicine remains but an unreachable ideal if the permanent formation of hospital staff in the ethic of virtue is lacking. It is this ethic of virtue which transforms hospital workers into individuals who are sensitive to human values and who promote humanising behaviours.

A humanising formation should involve all medical, nursing and administrative staff in order to reach all sections of the hospital and be embedded there. The humanising aspect of care is so important that it *should* involve the whole of the hospital community and have an impact on the whole environment, from the reception counter to the offices, the wards, operating theatres and the chaplaincy. Humanisation transforms the hospital and creates an atmosphere in which workers feel they belong to one family rather than being mere colleagues. Just as a doctor must consider the effects of treatment of a single organ on the whole body, so must all functionaries and workers who care for the sick take all human and social factors into consideration in order to aim for the greatest common good.[6]

It is therefore clear that humanisation must be the mission of *all* hospital workers, beginning with the way the receptionist or telephone operator answers patients' questions about appointments, visits, doctors, hospital stays and so on. Unfortunately, modern digital telephone answering machines have depersonalised calls: having been forced to listen to some minutes of music over the line, one is then asked to press different buttons according to whom one needs to reach. Aged patients calling from different towns or counties must be able to press the right numbers, after which, having got through to the hospital, they get a recorded message. This is certainly unsatisfactory, and does not make patients feel they are being given personal or humane treatment.

Hospital humanisation should be global: that means it should extend to all levels and not be limited to the chief medical officer or the nurses; even the catering staff who distribute food trays at meal times should avoid merely placing trays on tables and walking out without a word to the patients. When, fortunately rarely, I have happened upon this kind of wordless treatment, I have always felt the need to intervene. The least that can be said is 'Enjoy your meal', even if ideally the true 'samaritan' might ask the patient if the food on the tray is what has been ordered, and whether the patient is able to get off the bed and eat unaided. If the patient needs to be fed, the orderly should at the very least advise a nurse or volunteer helper of this.

ALL IT TAKES IS A CARESS
In relation to this, I remember the beautiful experience of a young Maltese seminarian who used to come to the hospital with his companions during summer holidays as a volunteer helper. It was all new to them, and they were full of zeal, enthusiasm and love for the sick.

On their first day a nurse asked the young seminarian to feed one of the elderly patients. This totally surprised the young man and he had no idea what to do. So the nurse showed him how to do it, saying, 'You've got to be very patient, but do it imagining he were your own father'. This is the proper attitude, and that seminarian, now a fully-fledged priest, never forgot that lesson in humanisation and love. It would be wonderful if all seminarians were to have such an experience.

It is such small gestures which endow a hospital with a humane and familiar environment, because the patient feels that he or she is among friends who care for him or her with gentleness and solicitude. Little things like a smile, a greeting, a caress, a listening ear, and perhaps an anecdote told, are all signs of a humanised environment. The patient deserves such treatment, being our brother or sister in Christ.

In his book *A Caress for Healing: The New Medicine, a Balance of Science and Conscience*, researcher and oncologist Professor Umberto Veronese states that 'a caress is worth more than a long discussion. A doctor, or better still, a good doctor, should never forget to put his patient at the centre, creating an authentic rapport with his patient, which helps form a bond of faith and dialogue'.

This is the essence of humanisation. Over the years I have received many very moving letters of thanks from former patients at the hospital for the humane way in which they had been treated by doctors and nurses who exuded love and joy, to the extent that they may be referred to as, in the words of St Paul, 'servants of our joy' as he called those who transmitted the Good News. Young nurses from Italy, the Philippines, Africa, Poland, Arab countries, Albania, China, Peru, Brazil – from thirty-five different countries – 'put their hands to the plough' without looking back, without stopping or wasting time and without ever being ill-mannered with patients. Undoubtedly, the hospital environment helps, and during the monthly meetings with new employees they are always reminded that the hospital expects high standards of care, which they should all aspire to reach. Each one is expected to be 'Top Gun'! This admonition is always met with a smile, but its message gets through. If one is not prepared to aim for the 'top', to give of one's best, then it would be better to leave the hospital's employ, for it only takes one rotten apple to spoil the barrel.

Clearly, humanisation depends on the character and helpfulness of the individual worker, since people of all ages, cultures, nations and religions work in a hospital. There co-exist a variety of ideologies and experiences: some are happily married; some single; some separated or divorced. In an ideal setting, all would be practising Catholics, but it often happens that hospital workers are not all believers: it all depends on the policies of the human resources office, which has to recruit staff selectively but without discrimination, as is done in all large companies. Some Lutheran and Jewish hospitals in the United States and Israel, for example, recruit only personnel who belong to their respective creeds. However, in a modern European pluralistic society, it is understandably difficult, even for a hospital of Christian inspiration, to recruit staff only among the faithful. Moreover, following such a policy could undermine the scientific professionalism of one's staff complement. I know medical chiefs who are unbelievers; Jewish, or non-Catholics, who faithfully respect the philosophy and ethics of the hospital where they work. They are true gentlemen, in the sense meant by Cardinal John Henry Newman, who converted to Catholicism from the Anglican Church while at Oxford, when he averred that before being Catholic, one needs to be a gentleman in order to respect other people's views. It is, however, vital that these professionals embrace the principles and ethos inspiring the structure within which they work, especially with regards to the ethics associated with the beginning and ending of human life and scientifically assisted fertilisation, and the Christian values on which the hospital's ethos is based. It would be the antithesis of ethical for any single employee to ignore or be disloyal to the hospital's fundamental principles.

The same applies to teaching staff of the university or the research departments. Lecturers who attempt to influence the students with philosophies or political ideas which are antithetical to the university statute cannot be tolerated. Sadly, lecturers sometimes slip into indiscretions, a fact which I have on occasion discovered from the students themselves.

HUMANISATION AND RESEARCH
Research is another minefield if one is not cognisant of one's limits and does not respect the fundamental values. Some non-Catholic research scientists who openly declared themselves agnostic or atheist in the press on the occasion of the Italian referendum on artificially assisted pregnancy and who work in Catholic research institutions have ranged themselves squarely and without reservations in favour of life and in defence of the fundamental human values as regards stem cell research and artificially assisted procreation. These are credible witnesses and true 'gentlemen'. There are others who, despite working within Christian research institutions, have not proved as faithful to the Christian values which inspire such institutions. It is my opinion that in matters concerning human life a *laissez-faire* attitude which allows each individual the freedom to behave according to his or her own conscience and sense of responsibility is unacceptable. On such issues, the organisation should furnish its workers with protocols and guidelines which must be faithfully adhered to.

Research should be aimed at curing and overcoming illnesses. However, unfortunately, what happens in Italy, unlike in other countries, is that scientific research is not always funded either by government or private corporations. For decades research has been undervalued, resulting in a brain drain as researchers have travelled abroad where, not only do they earn more, but they are given more opportunities and funding, and shown appreciation. Nowadays we are witnessing the return of a number of young Italian scientists with a wealth of foreign experience under their belts, which is extremely useful for Italy and to the advantage of the sick; especially since most of these researchers often have published articles to their credit in prestigious scientific journals like *Science, The Lancet* and *Nature*. Research helps humanise medicine through its new discoveries, although most of the hard work involved takes place behind the scenes and therefore goes unacknowledged.

At this point we may hypothesize the course of the humanisation of medicine and hospitals which involves all workers and the very institution in relation to the sick, both resident and outpatients, and to their families who are also victims of whatever illness their loved ones are afflicted with. There exist nowadays public relations offices attempting to promote humanisation through communication with patients, especially when medical errors take place, in cases where information is lacking and in instances of bad medical practice. This is not an easy task, and cannot be approached in a bureaucratic or technical manner, as experience has shown. It is a task which requires great human sensitivity founded on respect for the patient, succinctly defined by the English maxim 'the customer is always right'. These public relations offices are undoubtedly very helpful, but lose their *raison d' être* the moment they become a mere frontline defence of the hospital they serve. Despite the fact that these offices are not to be mistaken for patients' tribunals, those responsible should adopt an attitude of empathy with and unconditional acceptance of patients and never be negatively judgemental or prejudiced in favour of the hospital they represent. The latter attitude only serves to increase the patients' and their families' resentment, disillusionment and antagonism. The personnel working within public relations offices, only recently introduced in Italy, need to be specifically trained in public relations, personal communication and humanisation, as well as by nature being sensitive to the needs and feelings of others.

GOD IS LOVE

I shall conclude this chapter by recounting an episode involving the application of ethics. There was a great stir in the media following the death of a patient after an operation, due to an infection which could have put the lives of other patients at risk.

Her relatives, one of whom runs a private radio station, were understandably bitter, and threatened the hospital with legal action. It was difficult to placate them in order to explain that the death had not been caused by medical error. The surgeon was a highly qualified and humane person, but rather too outspoken. This was a case which necessitated a diplomatic choice of speech while still telling the truth. It was absolutely necessary to regain the family's trust, not by acting neutrally, but by nurturing a common understanding which would give way to dialogue and ultimately transparency. The spokesmen were the hospital lawyer and the patients' tribunal, and they were able to discuss the case with objectivity and negotiate an agreement. Thus an explosive situation was defused without involving the chief of staff, who had not been in the wrong in this case.

The arrangement satisfied all parties concerned, and the dispute was resolved without pain or offence to the family. It is therefore patent that administrators and functionaries must, just as much as doctors, consider the patient and his or her family as partners and brothers.

True humanisation is created solely through love, and the path to it is facilitated by the principle that *Deus Caritas est*, God is Love.[7]

By dedicating his first encyclical to the Church as a 'Community of Love', Benedict XVI has rendered a great service to humanity, and most especially to those who are suffering. He writes: 'At a time when vengeance and even the duty to commit violence and acts of hatred are associated with the name of God, this is a message of great relevance and tangible significance.'[8]

Like evangelisation, charity is the duty of the Church and of all Christians, for it is none other than the love of one's neighbour. Doctors and all health workers should be inspired and moved to act in a spirit of charity. Holy Communion (*koinonia*), the breaking of bread and prayer are the pillars on which the humanisation of a hospital is built. Healthcare is a 'deaconate' in the sense meant by the early Church, a 'ministry of charity'. As the Pope has written, it is 'the service of neighbourly love exercised communally and in an immediate context' and he goes on to say, 'it was fundamentally established in the very structure of the Church'.[9] From the middle of 'the fourth century this "deaconate" existed in Egypt, in the monasteries which were responsible for the whole gamut of activities involving aiding the sick, in fact, in charitable services'.[10]

As a symbol of humanisation and charity, the Pope places before us the model displayed in the parable of the Good Samaritan, according to which 'Christian charity is first and foremost simply the response to that which, in a given situation, constitutes the immediate need of the moment: the hungry need feeding; the naked need dressing; the sick need to be cared for until they are well; prisoners need to be visited, and so on ... Professional competence is a fundamental necessity, but it is not enough in dealing with the needs of human beings, who need that something more than technically correct treatment. They need humanity: they need attention from the heart'.[11]

NOTES

1 Cf. *Caring*, V.A. Ferrari (ed.), 2003, pp. 273–83.
2 Milan, 2003, p. 137.
3 Principles of the San Raffaele, Milan.
4 S. Leone, *The Theological Perspective in Bioethics*, ISB (Sicilian Bioethical Institute), Palermo, 2002.
5 Principles of the San Raffaele, Milan.
6 Cf. *Caring*, p. 246.
7 Jn 1:4, 8.
8 Benedict XVI, *Deus Caritas est*, I, Vatican Library, Vatican City, 2006.
9 Ibid., 21.
10 Ibid., 23.
11 Ibid., 31b.

CHAPTER 3

SOME BASIC PRINCIPLES OF ETHICS

Cecily Saunders cared very deeply for the sick in her care. She founded hospices in the UK for patients diagnosed with cancer, who were treated with great care and could live in a homely environment during the last months of their lives. She often said to them: 'We care deeply for you, simply because you are who you are. Your lives remain meaningful to the very end. We will do our utmost, not only to help you face death, but also to make sure you lead meaningful lives to the very end.'

When the young Jane Zorza learned she had a tumour she exclaimed, 'I am not ready to die'. Her father, Victor Zorza, described this in his book entitled *A Way to Die*.[1] Thanks to the hospice movement, in the months that followed Jane Zorza learned that death, contrary to what many believed, was not necessarily an experience to fear. Far from being, as many are apt to believe, a defeat, her death was a victory against both pain and fear. This discovery was a triumph both for Jane herself, and for all those who cared for her in the hospice.

This proved to be the outcome of the enormous good done by Saunders and others who, like her, are dedicated to the service of all who were afflicted with cancer. The sick who, incidentally, while in Saunders' care were never referred to as 'the terminally ill'. Yet another well-known and saintly person who dedicated her life to the care of the poor and sick was Mother Teresa of Calcutta, beatified by John Paul II.

A MEETING WITH MOTHER TERESA IN CALCUTTA

It was way back in 1962, when, still a very young priest, I set off for Calcutta in order to learn more about Mother Teresa and her wonderful work, carried out in the 'Home for the Dying'. Each day, babies, children, youths, as well as those who had reached an acute stage of their illness were received into this house, a former Hindu temple. Mother Teresa and her community of nuns greeted all the poor brought in off the streets with love and affection. She embraced them all without distinction, saying, 'They have lived like animals, now they can die like angels'. Her single burning desire was not the conversion of these 'poorest of the poor' but being of service to them to the very end of their lives. Her ardent wish was to 'do something beautiful for God and his children'. Her faith led her to believe that God himself would do the rest.

Both Cecily Saunders and Mother Teresa provide excellent examples of the correct ethical treatment of the sick centred around the respect for the human dignity of each person. Proper and ethical bedside manners practised daily are clearly manifested in hospital wards, in homes for the elderly, in hospices, and wherever else the suffering may be found. Care and love expressed at each bedside are transformed into dedication and compassion. Ethical treatment of the sick, as a consequence of this, becomes, like the practice of medicine, a sacred art, aimed at healing and caring for each human being as a whole.

It is at this present moment in time that ethical care must be put into practice. The worlds of science and technology cannot do without it. The challenges created by scientific knowledge in the life of each man, from the moment of his conception to the time of his death, can only find answers in an ethical treatment which upholds the fundamental values of the human person. In hospital aisles and wards, doctors and nurses question themselves daily regarding the best way of solving ethical problems which arise when dealing with various pathologies.

Scientific knowledge and an awareness of the correct ethical behaviour should go hand in hand when treating the sick. Both principles of scientific and theoretical ethics are the foundations which help create a deep sense of awareness of how best to treat patients. These principles ought to be taught in lecture rooms. Unfortunately, the teaching of the correct ethical procedures is very often absent in the education of medical students.

Action plans put forward by committees studying the proper forms of ethical treatment need to be put into practice. This, in turn, would be of great value when young doctors are faced with problems posed by science and medicine. In a pluralistic society, as ours is today, ethical problems can only be solved through confrontation and a Socratic dialogue. This is so apparent that one cannot talk of a unique or single 'ethical practice' but of diverse 'ethics'. Neither can one limit ethics to the mere consideration of whether or not a particular practice is licit, for such reasoning, besides being reductive, is also in itself anti-ethical.

JÉRÔME LEJEUNE'S TESTIMONY

The age-old contrasting differences between the Tree of Knowledge and the Tree of Life, as well as those between *homo sapiens* and *homo tecnologicus*, are very actual. This is so evident that man today must admit to experiencing two conflicting ideologies: the first being a knowledge of facts and the other being an awareness that mankind still very often faces uncertainties in life. The well-known geneticist who discovered Trisomy 21 (Down Syndrome), Jérôme Lejeune, once declared: 'The greater our knowledge of genetics and its influence on the mechanics of life itself, the lesser our knowledge of human nature and mankind itself.'

Pope John Paul II, on a visit to Paris, visited Lejeune's grave and stopped to pray there. Lejeune was a researcher, as well as a man of high moral standards. When once asked to exemplify his concepts, Lejeune, who had been called upon to act as a consultant, gave details of a case which occurred in Marysville, Tennessee. The case under scrutiny involved seven frozen embryos, the progenitors of which were about to separate. The mother wished to dispose of them by having them destroyed. Lejeune declared: 'A judge, like Solomon, had to decide if the embryos were simply "objects" to be protected or if they were, in fact, human beings.'

However, the divide between theoretical ethics and bedside ethics is rather marked. Very often ethical care is non-existent in hospitals, where the sick suffer. The situation is different, however, in foreign countries, among them the USA, where, in many hospitals, experts on ethical care who accompany consultants and other doctors on ward rounds, are called upon to use their expertise when the need arises. This is the best way to bring ethical care to the bedside. Today, in fact, medical care poses many questions. Doctors, nurses and even patients' own relatives search for solutions, which may determine the best possible methods of treating patients, as well as contributing to their total well-being.

Solutions offered by experts in ethical care are very often founded on philosophical and theological principles. Experts in the field of the ethical treatment of patients, and professors who teach ethics often hold meetings. Yet both groups often have no close contact with the sick or their suffering. They firmly believe that philosophical or anthropological texts can actually provide solutions to all problems that arise. What they both lack, however, is an understanding of human suffering borne of experience. Being at a distance from the sick, their perception of what healing and caring for them actually involves contains lacunae because it does not consider the 'person' as its focal point. Their ideas, thoughts and attitudes are often secular, and contrast with true human and Christian ethical values.

All who teach and talk of ethical values without ever having been in close contact with the sick often demonstrate a total lack of empathy and compassion towards the suffering. On occasion, the so-called 'experts' express opinions founded on philosophical concepts, on liberal, Marxist, relativistic ideals. Since the greater part of all communication networks available are, in reality, commercial enterprises, a number of lecturers are frequently given the opportunity of expressing their secular views to the general public in the press, and on radio and TV. They can also air their opinions in parliament, where topics such as abortion, divorce, in-vitro fertilization, homosexuality and marriage, which, in fact, are all closely dependent on ethical principles, are debated.

The knowledge of ethics alone is simply not enough. One needs to be guided by a conscientious approach to ethics. At this opportune moment, I shall quote what Giovanni Fornero wrote when introducing his book, *Catholic Bioethics and Secular Bioethics*: 'Some non-practising Catholics, as well as a number of scholars scarcely disposed to associate themselves with the doctrinal positions of the Magisterium of Popes John Paul II and Benedict XVI, tend to underestimate the bioethics pertaining to the sacredness of life.'[2]

It is at the bedside of a patient that one begins to learn the necessary and correct ethical behaviour. One should approach a patient with extreme care, with a respect that is, in itself, a manifestation of the love we bear for that person. 'Love thy neighbour as thyself' is the greatest of all commandments, but the love shown to a sick person is the greatest love of all. And this applies to believers as well as non-believers.

WHO IS MAN?

This vision stems from our understanding that God created human beings, each unique and singular, to his own image. The starting point in the study of anthropological ethics is 'mankind'. Such ethics, inherent in human nature, therefore should begin with mankind and be of service to man. The question that automatically follows such a statement is therefore: Who is Man? Speaking in philosophical terms, this question may be rephrased as 'What should "Man" mean to us?' Psalm 8 poses an identical question:

> Ah, what is man that you should spare a thought for him,
> the son of man that you should care for him?
>
> Yet you have made him little less than a god,
> you have crowned him with glory and splendour,
> made him lord over the work of your hands,
> set all things under his feet.[3]

These words of the Psalm clearly indicate that man, of all God's creatures, is endowed with dignity. We also find confirmation that man's very nature was God-given. God wished his only Son to become man and be born of a woman. His son, Jesus Christ, was born to a woman, namely the Virgin Mary. For this very reason we may claim to have the same genetic code as Jesus Christ.

Humanising care must be based on a holistic concept of the person – that is, body, psyche and soul – and on the total well-being of the individual (in our case, one who is suffering illness). In such cases one must perforce ask, 'Who should Man be to the doctor and to other health workers?' The question we must then ask ourselves is, 'How can we, ultimately, define the word "Man"?' The starting point is, without doubt, the sanctity of the life of each individual and unique person. When encountering a sick person, especially one who is facing death, we should bear in mind that his life has been full of experiences, some of beauty or sorrow, some of darkness or light. The patient may be unknown to us and, at that moment in time, his illness may seem a nightmare, and death a taboo. Yet, at that moment in time a chaplain who can offer hope, comfort and spiritual guidance is often kept as far away from the room as possible, so as not to cause the patient to feel alarmed, or even so as not to upset members of the patient's family!

In today's pluralistic society, the ethics of the Catholic Church are diametrically opposed to the ethical guidelines upheld by the secular world and we cannot obstinately cling to strictly Christian ethics. We should, rather, be prepared to listen to and consider more secular ideas, without necessarily relinquishing our own principles, and it follows that we expect the same treatment. However, there is very often a total lack of Socratic dialogue and a true and meaningful exchange of ideas between the Church and secular society. I personally experienced this during my years in charge of organising seminars for the European Bioethics Day in Milan. Both Catholic and secular experts had always been invited to participate, in the hope that a certain intellectual and professional equilibrium would be maintained. This lasted until a small number of non-Catholics decided to take over the organisation of the seminars, following which the balanced exchange of Catholic and secular ideas disappeared and I had no choice but to discontinue the organisation of such seminars.

We must put a stop to all forms of sarcasm, divisions and ostentatious superiority on all sides, and resume discussion. The single factor which unites the two (or more) ethical ideologies is man, since we all believe in man's dignity, personality, freedom, rights and responsibilities. We must respect one another's opinions since there is more that unites than which keeps us apart (Blessed Pope John XXIII).

CORRECT CLINICAL PRACTICE

For seven years I was a member of the European Council's bioethical committee (CAHBI) in Strasbourg. When debating the European Charter on Bioethics, although conflicting views were often voiced (for example on topics such as the embryo, stem cells, euthanasia and so on), all the participants were united by an ethical consciousness that made mankind and human values their point of departure. The same ethical spirit has always guided and been a strong unifying factor for the two ethics committees, namely the Milan National Cancer Institute and the European Oncological Institute, run by Professor Umberto Veronesi, of which I formed part for fifteen years. Despite being the only clerical ethicist present, I often agreed totally with the secularist views expressed. Even when we were not in total agreement, we still believed whole-heartedly in the ethical values of man, his rights, liberty and dignity. This was proof of our shared commitment to guarantee the respect due to mankind, in accordance with the European Council's proposals regarding social justice and equality for all (European Council 1991).[4]

Within hospitals there should never be differences of opinion, either in practical matters or in the spiritual culture, of Catholic ethics and the ethical ideas belonging to secularists, because practice is part and parcel of spirit, and vice versa.[5] This ideal should unite the two worlds (Catholic and secular) with all medical professionals caring for the sick in a shared brotherhood at the service of the sick, treating patients without any discrimination towards colour, race or creed. It is in this spirit and with this attitude that we should *live* bedside ethics, like a team which communicates and collaborates, because care and treatment cannot be left to single individuals. Treatment works better, and bears more fruit when the workers involved have an ethical conscience which accompanies patients in their suffering and shares their hopes of a cure. Pope John Paul II reminds us that 'Being at the service of man imposes upon us an obligation to vociferously declare that *we must never ignore the fundamental rules of ethics*, no matter how valid new scientific discoveries, especially in the field of biotechnology, may be'.[6]

I do not believe there is a need for me to go deeper into the correct definition of ethics: it is only necessary for me to give a clear picture of what a personalised ethical treatment should be.

Ethics is the science of behaviour and moral values. It analyses the theories of moral thought. It allows us to formulate an ethical judgement, regarding what would be most correct for the well-being of each individual and what, on the other hand, would cause the most harm simply because it is not permissible.

In the context of this present work, these moral and ethical theories are applied to the practice – assistance, care, therapy, treatment, surgery etc. – of medicine, and in the application of research protocols. In order to exercise good clinical practice according to the Helsinki Declaration, the doctor is ethically obliged to follow these principles.

New technology, the progress achieved through research, the actual cost of medical care, new legislation and patients' high expectations have, all together, created an awareness of the importance of knowledge and understanding in the practice of medical ethics today. Each doctor must implement medical ethics aiming at the total well-being of each person and at a better quality of life, from the moment of conception to death.

UNIVERSAL ETHICAL PRINCIPLES

The universally accepted ethical principles reflect the following:

(a) *Autonomy:* Years ago, doctors, using a paternalistic approach, made the required decisions, believing that they knew what was best for their patients. However in today's world the patient is the protagonist throughout his illness and, as such, has the right to be consulted when any decisions regarding his medical treatment are taken.

(b) *Benevolence:* Translated into other terms this means 'a desire to do good', 'to do one's best'; to provide the best possible treatment when caring for the sick, when offering cures, planning pain-relief treatment, when operating and even while offering intensive therapy. All doctors and nurses should have one common aim – doing their best for the benefit of each of their patients.

(c) *Do no harm:* Doctors must at all times remember their solemn Hippocratic oath. They must never harm their patients nor, directly or indirectly, cause injury.

(d) *Faithfulness* to the code of ethics recommended by good clinical practice. Faithfulness to the code of ethics involves: a regard for the dignity of each individual, and for his right to privacy; professional confidentiality; telling the patient the truth about his condition; constant monitoring and care of the patient, and humanisation.

(e) *Social and Collective Justice:* All individuals, no matter their class, wealth, colour, race or creed, share the same rights.

(f) *Benefits:* Justice demands that treatment offered should be calculated on the principles of cost and benefits and that no sums of money should be frittered away.

(g)   *Spiritual care:* All medical treatment should treat a patient in a holistic manner, i.e. healing body, mind and spirit. It is a duty to provide patients with spiritual help in all private and public Catholic hospitals.

I have always maintained, as we shall see ahead, that committees on ethics have both the responsibility and the duty to ensure that these ethical principles are put into practice by all medical staff. These ethical principles must also form part of the permanent teaching given to doctors, medical students and nurses.

Since the assistance given to the sick must be holistic, the ethical care offered to a patient must perforce be three dimensional: medical, psychological and spiritual. In each hospital ward the services of three professionals is required: that of a doctor, a psychologist and a chaplain. Bearing in mind a patient's ethical rights, the three, working as a team, would strive towards giving each patient the best possible quality of life. In essence, it is this 'type' of care that should characterise the relationships between the staff, patients and their families. In an introduction to his medical textbook Harrison affirms that to achieve humanisation 'it is vital that each doctor realises the importance of putting the patient and his family at ease, assuring them that all that could possibly have been done, has been done'. This statement must of course be a truthful one.

Achieving this 'type' of ethical care requires a radical change of heart and mind, since it is very often we ourselves, our attitudes and manners, which are the greatest obstacles in the way of its happening.

The main character in the novel *Lazarus,* by the well-known Catholic author Morris West, is a fictitious pope, Leo XIV, who must undergo a cardiac bypass. The heart specialist performing the operation is a Jew. In the weeks following surgery the pope is given psychological support by a brilliant, beautiful and pleasant Swedish cardiologist. Her overwhelming empathy is such that the pope experiences a 'change of heart' and becomes more receptive to and conscious of the misery, suffering and frailty of all mankind. After experiencing this close doctor-patient relationship, the pope starts to work on creating radical reforms in the Church.

Change and humanisation in hospital care can only be the result of a change of heart. Future doctors and nurses, that is, present medical and nursing students must aspire to achieving this change of heart: they must become rich in ethical virtues – young men and women who are sensitive not only to the medical, physical needs of their patients but also to their psychological and spiritual needs, because the curing of the sick is a *sacred* mission.

NOTES

1   V. Zorza, *A Way to Die*, Edizioni Paoline, Cinisello Balsamo (MI), 1984, p. 11.

2   G. Fornero, *Catholic Bioethics and Secular Bioethics*, Mondadori, Milan, 2005, p. x.

3   *The Jerusalem Bible*, Psalm 8.

4   Cf. *Aver Cura*, p. 34.

5   Cf. *Aver Cura*, p. 4, cited by Fr L.M. Verzè.

6   Apostolic Letter 51, *Novo millennio ineunte*, John Paul II, Vatican Library, Vatican City, 2001.

CHAPTER 4

THE PATIENT AND 'I': A RELATIONSHIP BASED ON HELP

It all started, many years ago, in the mid-1950s: I was a young priest, and had just ended a seven-year period of study at the Gregorian Pontifical University and the Venerable English College, in Rome. I was then in Chicago, the guest of a dynamic Irish parish priest. He often boasted of his friendship with Al Capone, who had provided the wine used in the celebration of Mass during the years of prohibition. At eight o'clock one morning, an Ash Wednesday, the parish priest assigned me to visit Mary, a twenty-year-old cancer patient whose death was fast approaching. The parish priest's words were: 'Try to cheer her up. She needs courage to face what's coming.'

I approached Mary with a certain degree of diffidence. The hospital room was small, bare, and in semi-darkness. Mary was young, pale and blonde, barely visible among the white sheets between which she lay. I spoke to her, chatting at some length about Rome, the Pope, St Peter, the Trevi fountain full of coins thrown in by tourists. I realised that, though Mary listened, her mind was elsewhere.

At one point she reached out and, taking my hand, asked, 'Father, are you afraid of dying?' Words failed me. Being so young and inexperienced I could neither find the words nor the strength to answer a question I had never thought of asking myself. I stood there dumbfounded, sweat rolling down my face, my hands cold, my fear and embarrassment obvious. Not having had an answer, Mary said, 'Father, please talk to me about dying'. I felt a sudden urge to cry, and longed to make my escape. After a hurried blessing, I made a rapid retreat from the room. Nobody, throughout my seven years at university, had spoken to me about death, and neither had they prepared me to answer such questions. All I had been taught was how to correctly administer the sacrament then called 'Extreme Unction', the anointing of the sick with sacred oils.

Panic-stricken, I rushed out of the hospital desiring to speak to the parish priest. Facing him squarely, I said, 'I do not know how a priest should assist the sick'. He reassured me, saying I would eventually overcome my fears and sense of impotence. His advice was that I should act as naturally as possible and pray to St Jude Thaddeus, a saint I had barely heard of at the time, who was the patron saint of cancer patients. I must frankly admit that at that time I was quite unable to feel any sort of compassion. Instead I was filled with anger. How could God have permitted such a beautiful, clever, twenty-year-old to be struck down by such an awful illness? I lacked faith, but, clearly, my prayers to St Jude were beneficial. I fought on. I visited Mary in hospital every day for about a month. Ever so gradually, my fear of death faded. I spoke to the young patient about what death, according to our Christian faith, implies. I did this to strengthen her faith, but in actual fact it was my own that was fortified. I sat with Mary, who was clearly grateful for this, praying with her and offering her consolation till she breathed her last.

In reality this proved to be my first lesson about life itself. I grew to know myself better, finding within me an ability to empathise with the sick and their families. I realised I possessed the spiritual resources which allowed me, for the future, to assist many friends as well as the sick in hospitals when their deaths were imminent. When I talk of ethical care, which is so vital in helping the sick, I think of Mary. It was she who had filled my heart with a desire to assist the sick and who helped me understand what suffering, sickness and death really mean. I shall be eternally grateful to Mary and still thank her each day.

KNOWLEDGE OF ONESELF

The above experience can help us comprehend that it is our desire to be personally involved which gives an impetus to each of our relationships with the sick. It is only via self-knowledge that we realise that loving the sick is, in actual fact, loving oneself. Who am I when I face the sick? How do I empathise with the illness of others? These are fundamental questions which must be answered in order to put into practice a Catholic or secular ethical treatment of the sick. Unless one can find answers to these questions, one cannot really help the suffering.

This is what I learned from Carl Rogers, in Chicago, when I studied person-centred therapy. Carl Rogers defined self-knowledge as an 'insight' or 'introspection'. Coherence and authenticity are both vital inherent qualities required if one is to achieve self-awareness. Only after one has attained this should one consider becoming a doctor, nurse, psychologist or priest. One must first master the skills of positive thinking and communication that help create a valid relationship with each patient. We each have, within ourselves, an inherent human knowledge of ethical care, but only after effectively using our potential awareness can we help others. Our human frailty and even a negative outlook may be the spurs which urge us towards finding the strength to help others, especially if this means being able to help the sick. If we learn how to question ourselves and work harder so as to bring about the necessary changes within ourselves, we will become more humane and valid professionals.

As far as doctors and nurses are concerned, this journey of self-discovery should begin during their years of study, through personal training. Throughout my years teaching ethics I used the following method: first I would teach the principles of ethical care, then I would teach the applied theory. In fact, it was only after I had begun to learn more about myself that I found the strength to allow myself to wholly comprehend and be engulfed in Mary's pain and illness. I was at first completely unaware of this, and my escape from Mary's room was provoked by my inability to face such pain. I then thought of Christ himself, our doctor and healer, who 'bore our sufferings and carried our sorrows'.[1] It was only then that I began to think of Mary as my 'sister', or better still, as my 'spiritual daughter', as we are reminded by Isaiah's words: 'Because you are precious in my eyes, because you are honoured and I love you.'[2]

It is through self-awareness that we can accept ourselves as we are. My being incapable of answering Mary's question filled me with self-contempt and I then even doubted if I would ever be able to carry out my duties at the bedside of a patient. A person who believes he is incapable or unable to fulfil his duties automatically finds difficulty in accepting himself 'as he truly is' (Carl Rogers). As a result of this, he cannot even accept others. One's refusal to accept one's own limitations makes relationships with others difficult to achieve. Neither must we be disconcerted or disheartened by our own weaknesses, negative attitudes and imperfections. Even though our ultimate goal should be the attainment of perfection – 'Be perfect as your Heavenly Father is perfect' – God accepts us as we are: far from perfect beings who do their best to help other imperfect beings.

In this way, all involved in healthcare can acquire an ethical conscience since it is a knowledge of oneself which strengthens one's insight, behaviour and the ability to form relationships. When one does not have an ethical conscience it is easy to fall into the trap of relativism. It is clarity of mind and spirit which enables us to be more honest and coherent when dealing with the sick, for too much talk will do nothing to help. At this junction, the words of St Paul come to mind: 'My grace is enough for you: my power is at its best in weakness.'[3]

All health workers must attempt to deepen their knowledge of self in order to transmit their serenity to the sick and be accepted by them, otherwise they may very soon experience a crisis and reach what psychologists term 'burn-out'. Even though counselling teaches us the theory of non-involvement and the distancing of ourselves from patients, we cannot always ignore our feelings.

AWARENESS OF ONE'S FEELINGS

Healthcare workers must be aware of their own feelings and learn how to manage them. In order to do so it is necessary for them to ask themselves the following questions:

1. How can I control my feelings when facing these situations?
2. What is my own attitude towards death?

3.   How can I reconcile certain behaviour in hospitals and the ensuing injustices?

I agree with the well-known psychoanalyst Robert Carkuff when he claims that one must know how a carer feels vis-à-vis the sick.[4] Even when in the middle of a crisis, the sick are fully aware of what is happening around them. They are conscious of what doctors, nurses, chaplains, and even members of their own family, are thinking. That is the reason why each carer must control his emotions, so as to transmit a sense of peace and tranquillity, rather than one of agitation. Despite the fact that the patient may be suffering, and because he is lying in bed we may discount that he is aware of those around him, he is nonetheless sensitive to the moods and emotions of the people around. Any emotional stress, even if silent, which we show at that moment can disturb and agitate a patient and cause him to lose all hope.

One foreign psychotherapist, a woman of great faith who was a member of the Charismatic Movement and had a great love and a deep compassion for the sick, said, 'In each of the sick I see Christ'. However, she often cried and allowed her emotions to get the better of her when facing the sick. This eventually led to a burn-out and she was forced to retire.

Carkuff clearly points out which qualities should be necessary in all those who work with and accompany the sick. The required qualities are: a sincere concern for others; tolerance and an ability to accept people whose opinions differ from one's own; a healthy regard for self; human warmth and a sensibility when dealing with others as well as an ability to empathise with them.[5]

These qualities must be taken very seriously. A 'healthy regard for self' is such an important objective that Christ himself commanded us to love ourselves before loving our neighbour. The word 'healthy' is the opposite of fragile, weak, egocentric, needy, or cold. If a person is not healthy in mind, body or spirit, he or she may give off negative vibes that can harm the sick. Moreover, one must also be very aware of one's own strengths, as well as one's limitations and weaknesses.

One must also be prepared to accept criticism from others; to work under the guidance of a supervisor or tutor; to accept oneself with the greatest tranquillity and peace of mind. Each of us has good qualities like generosity, kindness and loyalty, as well as negative traits such as jealousy, anger and wickedness. All these qualities influence our behaviour and attitudes when we deal with others. A doctor, when in a good mood, is often willing to listen attentively to his patients; when not, his behaviour may suggest a lack of humanity.

A young person who chooses to study medicine must be prepared to be at the service of the sick to cure, alleviate suffering and improve the lives of those in his or her care. He or she may mature, through the passing years, by means of further study, clinical practice and research, but must steadfastly maintain the motivation, ideals and belief in medicine. An overriding desire for personal gain or ambition to further one's career placed before the primary aim of being of service to others may easily lead to burn-out.

THE SICKBED AS A PLACE OF LEARNING

The Dalai Lama, whom I met in Milan and invited to visit the San Raffaele, often insisted, quite correctly, that we must work towards reducing our negative forces while seeking to strengthen the positive. This requires a constant reassessment of our lives in relation to others and a constant personal commitment to acquire self-control. It is only in this way that we can begin to know our own positive qualities better. These inherent resources are a constant help when dealing with others in hospitals. If doctors and nurses do not share this point of view and fail to give of their best to care for patients in a holistic manner, they are therefore reduced to being mere professionals or technicians who are detached from true life. The same applies to the ethicist who limits himself only to the subject at an academic level, without ever experiencing the practice of ethics at a bedside. Carers who may easily fall into this trap would soon realise that they are unable to look their patients in the eye.

A patient's bedside is, in itself, the greatest of all lecture theatres – the patient himself a living example of suffering, the greatest of all teachers. It is from patients that we learn about the significance of life, suffering, pain and death, just as I learned from being at Mary's bedside. Patients help their carers become better individuals, as well as giving them the opportunity to discover that dignity within themselves, rooted in Judaeo-Christian culture. One may say that patients help carers who are believers comprehend that the value of human life is, in fact, founded on God's vision. Non-believers, on the other hand, may be led to acknowledge that there exist superior and nobler values than those acquired through human reason alone.

The better we know ourselves, the easier it is for us to learn more about our patients and other people. Our efforts to offer each of the sick in our care a personalised ethical treatment gives credit to our ability to accept patients unconditionally, whether they be rich or poor, young or old, believers or not, easy to please or demanding. It is our duty to get to know each patient intimately and understand his unspoken needs. In every ward, one may come across – as I did – good-natured patients, anti-clericals who refuse all contact with priests, as well as those who accept their suffering and illness.

This learning process helps us better understand the intrinsic value of human nature. The Judaeo-Christian vision allows us to see a child of God in each patient, redeemed by Christ's passion and made victorious by his resurrection. In this light, each patient becomes a 'Son of God'. The Jesuit James Schall declares, 'the essence of civilization, ethics and dignity [of man] is the following: all life, even that of a child with Down Syndrome – or any other medical condition – deserves to be lived'.[6]

As I have already pointed out, the above brings to light the beliefs held by the Blessed Mother Teresa of Calcutta, during the war between Israel and the PLO, in 1982. Working in that war zone, Mother Teresa and other nuns were doing their best to evacuate both mentally and physically disabled children from the devastated region of Sabra, where the Israeli bombings had caused havoc. It has been said that Mother Teresa uttered the following words: 'We must admit the war is evil. I do not understand what is happening. We are all children of God. Why are they doing this? I do not understand.' In her eyes, as well as in the eyes of doctors and nurses, any old, incontinent patient who calls out in pain and moans, is 'the Son of God', and as such should be treated with the same reverence and veneration that Christ's body would be treated with. I witnessed this occurring in a colony where Mother Teresa kissed and hugged all the lepers.

JOB AND SUFFERING

Many patients, amongst whom was a learned non-believer, were my mentors through the time when I was learning to know myself, both as a person and as a hospital worker. In the early days of my career I approached patients with a desire to help and be of use. I entered each room hoping to encourage patients. I felt that I was a Good Samaritan. However, very soon, my attitude changed. After meeting a patient and listening to him for a while, I became aware that it was each suffering patient who was making the effort to make me feel at ease. I understood then that should I want to be a good Samaritan, I had to begin to believe that each of the sick in fact represented the suffering Christ. From that moment on I usually left a bedside feeling humbled by each person's pain. It was this humility that helped me deepen my self-knowledge.

The well-known *Commentary to Job*, begun by St Gregory the Great when he lived in the community among his brother monks, and continued until the time when he was elected Pope, is a great account of hope emanating from his words which truly announce a 'new world' and 'new heavens'.[7]

Lactantius, a Father of the Church who died circa AD 330, believed that Epicurus had captured the true meaning of suffering in his work *De ira Dei* (On the Wrath of the Gods) and cites the four possible answers to the question of suffering and to the questions 'Why?' and 'Why me?' The biblical scholar Archbishop Gianfranco Ravasi summarises the text with the following remarks:

- *If God wants to do away with evil but cannot*, he is impotent. This does not tally with our concept of God.

- *If he can eradicate evil but will not,* then he is hostile towards us. This is yet another statement vilifying the image of God.
- *If he wishes to eliminate evil and can do so,* why then does evil exist? Why does he not eliminate it?[8]

Doctors and health workers do not limit themselves to making a diagnosis: they often experience the driving force of hope which enables a patient to overcome all difficulties and find a new world of hope. We are all 'sick' and we all bear the scars of 'wounds' such as egocentricity, carnal passions, a lack of charity etc. All require 'treatment'. If doctors and nurses treat patients humanely they will soon discover that the patient they are dealing with can 'cure' them. It is the sick who help medical staff fulfil their vocations and carry out their missions in the brotherly service of their patients. In such relationships it is the patients who perform the greater good.

Every patient is truly *Jesus, Deus Patiens* (Jesus, the suffering God), which are the words inscribed on the tabernacle in the churches both of the San Raffaele Hospital, dedicated to the Madonna of Life in Milan and Bahia, Brazil. Christ is present in the suffering of all the sick. He works within each of them. In the hospital that is also a temple are celebrated the 'rite of suffering' and that of love at the bedside of each patient, who should be provided with 'the most humane and medically sound surroundings, just like Christ's golden tabernacle'.[9]

The sick help us throughout the course of our lives, especially in a spiritual sense. We discover that Christ, our healer, works in the depths of our hearts. Hospital workers who believe in Christ and keep him in their hearts and minds are blessed with a special strength and are therefore more able to carry out their professional duties. This does not only occur with believers in the Catholic faith, as I realised when I worked alongside doctors and scientists who, despite being non-believers, proved to be extremely caring. Christ is present in every medical attempt to help the sick and it is he who cures the sick. Mother Teresa was fond of saying, 'I am simply a tool in the hands of God', and saints like Giovanni Calabria always considered themselves impotent without God's help. It is Christ who cures all and it is the strength of our spiritual values that gives us the energy and strength to carry out our medical professions and help cure the sick.

Human values, strengthened by a fervent belief in spiritual values, allow carers to share in each patient's suffering and hope for survival. Patients long to be treated with love and compassion. The Capuchin Saint Pio of Pietrelcina often urged doctors who worked in the Home for the Relief of Suffering to give a great dose of love together with their medicine. The ability to treat the sick not only with medication, but also with love is only possible if carers believe in spiritual values.

The Neapolitan doctor Saint Giuseppe Moscati, canonised by Pope John Paul II, conveyed his deep love for all those he treated. He had understood that his medical profession was, in fact, a mission at the service of the sick. His ideal was to serve God whenever he treated the sick, soothing the pains which afflict humanity, doing his utmost to help all the sick, especially those who were poor. His motto was: 'Science alone is not enough; if we want to transform the world we must act with honesty and love.' What a lesson for all doctors, especially those who do not practise their medicine as a vocation! And there are so many of these!

Doctors today and in the future must be persons of high moral fibre: people who understand the value of ethical care. They should not merely comply with the ethical practices imposed upon them by their profession. They must also carry out their duties with a greater love, due to the nature of their relationship with the sick.

DOCTORS OF THE FUTURE

This relationship must never be paternalistic. Doctors must refrain from being arrogant and authoritative. Patients are to be treated with respect because it is they who are the protagonists, and they have rights which must be safeguarded. Despite the fact that the patient lying in bed or sitting in an armchair is physically below the doctor, forced to look up to him, he or she should never be disregarded or treated anti-ethically, without consideration.

The authors Edmund D. Pellegrino, of the Kennedy Institute of Ethics in Washington, and David C. Thomasma, of Loyola University, Chicago, describe future doctors as 'those who are most able to acquire a patient's trust; who act with a recognisable professionalism; who are courageous, as well as honest, as the law requires; who are wise and prudent. They must also be individuals whose behaviour is professionally correct in their private, medical and social life'.[10] It therefore follows that doctors, nurses and carers must first of all have a favourable disposition before they contemplate practising the medical profession.

Monsignor Ronald Knox, who like Newman converted to Catholicism at Oxford, described this topic in a detailed work entitled *Enthusiasm*. Knox maintained that 'gentlemen', in our case carers, must be cheerful and possess a sense of humour. Doctors, nurses and ward sisters should smile and be cheerful when speaking to patients. Cardinal Joseph Ratzinger wrote: 'All those who believe in the Crucifixion of Christ and fully comprehend the grace they have acquired because of it should be joyful. A profound belief in the Cross makes resurrection a reality, renews our world and fills our hearts with joy.'[11]

NOTES

1 Isa 53:4.
2 Ibid., 43:4.
3 2 Cor 12:9.
4 R. Carkuff, *Helping and Human Relations: a Primer for Lay and Professional Helpers*, Chicago, 1969, pp. 184–7.
5 Ibid., pp. 11–16.
6 James Schall SJ, 'Surgical Death', in *Linacre Quarterly*, 49 (November 1982), 307.
7 E. Gandolfo, Gregorio Magno, *Gregory the Great, Servant of the Servants of God*, Vatican Library, Vatican City, 1988, p. 5.
8 *Medical-Priesthood Movement*, ed. A. Anzani, Scientific Institute, San Raffaele University Hospital, Milan, 2004, pp. 158–9.
9 Principles of the San Raffaele, Milan.
10 *For the good of the Patient*, Pauline Publications, Cinisello Balsamo (MI), 1992.
11 *Servants of Your Joy*, Àncora, Milan, 2002, p. 56.

Chapter 5

PERSPECTIVES WHICH FOSTER GOOD DOCTOR-PATIENT
RELATIONSHIPS

I was the victim of two accidents. One occurred in Catania, more than thirty years ago; the other in Milan five years ago, on the day following my return from Gaza, where I had witnessed the warfare. I beg pardon for including such personal details, but unfortunately it is such events that make lasting impressions on us.

All I clearly remember is the violent crash, the siren of the ambulance, the pain, the curious crowds and finally reaching the A&E department of the hospital. On both occasions, the minute I had been lowered, on a stretcher, out of the ambulance, I had heard a voice shouting out: 'Take him away! There's no place for him here! Leave!'

I recall feeling worthless, having been refused aid in the most uncivil, ill-mannered and, above all, unethical way. This was certainly not a manifestation of 'person-centred ethics' but a cruel example of how some healthcarers display a lack of humanity. In a way I was reminded of the priest who appears in the parable of the Good Samaritan as one of the passers-by, who did not stop to help the wounded and sick traveller, but had looked at him and walked on.

It is vital that we identify the attitudes that can facilitate our relationships with the sick. The method of doing so is that delineated by Carl Rogers, who advocated that all treatment should be centred around the sick individual.

'KNOWING' TO 'KNOW HOW TO ACT'

All carers and consultants should aim to create a method of treating patients which proves to be constructive. This does not simply mean learning a technique or a new form of communication. It is a skill acquired through practice and dynamic training: role play, communication and group work. It is in this way that we have trained many well-known consultants, psychologists, social workers and counsellors.

Carl Rogers' methods of acquiring a more profound self-awareness allows professionals, doctors and nurses to obtain not only the necessary knowledge of how to treat the sick, but – this is the most important factor of all – also teaches them to understand, accept and acknowledge their own personal identities. Rogers often repeated the sentence, 'I am who I am'; and 'person-centred therapy is a way of being an agreeable person' in interpersonal relations. 'In my relations with others I have learnt who I was not: I committed my greatest errors while trying to be somebody who was not myself.' It is futile for any professional, especially a doctor, to pass himself off as a specialist or expert in a field when this is not the case. Very often, the listener, even if merely a patient, realises this is not so, and it is then that professionals lose credibility.

When a patient asks to speak to a doctor or a nurse, it is often a need to be comforted that is being expressed by means of a more tangible request for medical attention. Sometimes the question is explicit, as in, 'Doctor, could you please check my blood pressure?' At other times patients are rather vague about what they want because they themselves do not realise that what they are truly after is the reassurance of communication with another human being. It is very important for all doctors and nurses to listen sensitively to patients and ask themselves what is truly being required of them. It is only when and if doctors do all of this and treat their patients as 'partners' that they can fulfil the true needs of their patients. The sick, who are afraid and anxious, and who, on occasion, refuse even to acknowledge the reality of their illness, are often quite unable to ask for the help they need. Some patients are vague; others use medical terms they may have heard on television. In such cases, one must be able to listen respectfully to the patient and then reach a conclusion about the illness. After having listened to their patients and assessed their needs, doctors should then gradually and discreetly communicate the truth about the illness. In order to help patients understand and accept this truth, doctors must show sensitivity and comprehension and, finally, offer hope.

At this point in time, the greatest of all assets is the humaneness with which doctors treat their patients. Pope John Paul II, in a speech to Catholic doctors, said: 'The humanisation of medicine is a proclamation of human dignity, respect for the body, for the spirit and the culture of each patient. In concrete terms, none of you can limit yourselves to being doctors who cure only the body but must care for the person as a whole, and even more than that, must foster relationships with each of your patients in order to make a valuable contribution to their well-being.'[1]

When a consultant or doctor transmits this kind of concern for and interest in his or her patients, he or she gains their trust and respect, even if the doctor is young. On the contrary, doctors who do not take on the responsibility of treating the total 'persona' do not inspire trust in their patients. They may even, in some cases, lose credibility.

When counselling, Virginia Satir points out: 'I am not an omnipotent God. Neither am I a parent or judge. The difficulty is to be professional without seeming to assume such qualities.'

THE PATIENT'S FEARS

On arrival in hospital a patient is often anxious. His anxiety may reach dramatic levels while he, and all those who have accompanied him, wait for his number to appear on the monitor. Elisabeth Kübler Ross describes the five levels of anxiety each patient experiences.[2]

The patient anxiously awaits test results. He has often no knowledge of why tests have been carried out, simply because nobody has bothered to explain it to him. He hears new terms in the diagnostic jargon with which he is unfamiliar (biopsy, endoscopy, MRI, electrocardiogram, angiogram etc.). He might have heard these terms used on TV medical programmes, but has probably never taken any special interest in them, simply because they did not hitherto concern him.

On occasion, patients are obliged to wait a day or so before being given a diagnosis. This only makes matters worse. They grow even more uneasy, begin to wonder what is to happen next, and sometimes panic. The words 'tumour', 'leukaemia' cross their minds. If, indeed, it is a tumour, where is it located? Even if doctors have tried to set their minds at rest and given them correct scientific explanations, patients are beset by a multitude of questions. They feel trapped, they fear the truth and even reject the possibility of survival.

This very often happens to the elderly who have never experienced serious illness and consequently have never been admitted into hospital. I remember well my own father who, aged seventy-three, during a visit to London, finally agreed to see the well-known Doctor Parker in Harley Street. Because my father had been fit and active and had never had a day of illness in his life, it required the intervention of the Holy Spirit to convince him to do this. The doctor came straight to the point: my father was told he had a tumour which required immediate surgery. What was so surprising at the time was how calmly and serenely my father reacted to this news which, in truth, alarmed me. The specialist, in a most humane and gentle way, gave him a comprehensible explanation and drew detailed diagrams which clearly showed what would be done during the operation. My father was heartened by this approach and, putting all his faith in the doctor, exclaimed: 'What a fine gentleman!'

Clearly it is only the doctor involved – I repeat, only the doctor – who can alleviate the fear, anxiety and terror that overcome patients. It is the very first step on the road to achieving a holistic treatment: patients must have complete faith and a total belief in their doctor.

In his book *Faith and Healing*, Ignazio R. Marino clearly indicates exactly what it is that patients expect from doctors: 'A patient's expectations are very high. To begin with, patients feel they should be able to confide in and trust another person who, in turn, should be able to help them and resolve their problems. Patients believe doctors should be accessible to them, trustworthy and sure of themselves. Patients will not accept negative answers ... People's faith in the progress of medicine is such that they often refuse to accept the limitations which unfortunately still exist.'[3]

EXPRESSING ONE'S FEELINGS

Each individual has feelings. The word 'feelings' goes far beyond merely denoting a person's intimate sentiments. As I have already pointed out, our feelings are only the tip of the iceberg. A child may cry and a sick person may call out, because both experience pain, which is what makes them do so. It is vital, therefore, for doctors to diagnose, or at least understand what, in fact, is causing the pain.

Understanding our own feelings furthers our self-knowledge. Our emotions bring to light our most intimate selves as well as life itself. At times we refuse to acknowledge and accept our feelings. We may even, on occasion, be ashamed of what we feel, and do our very best to smother our feelings. We may feel threatened by them, and consequently we put on a façade, or adopt some kind of defence mechanism.

Patients very often cry out in pain or fear. They are confused, uncertain and hardly logical. I have flared up when some patients have refused to accept their sickness. This has happened with patients who are ashamed of their illness or who have lost faith in their doctors, because they feel they have not been given enough attention. I firmly believe it is necessary for doctors both to expect and to accept such temporary outbursts. I believe that at such moments doctors should wait calmly, silently and impartially for the storm to blow over, yet, at the same time, with a kind look or a caress they should show their patients they understand. Since doctors can neither ignore nor reduce their patients' suffering, the next best treatment is keeping an eye on them, showing empathy towards them, as well as being as close to them as possible. Wounds cannot be healed by words – what is necessary is a sharing of sentiments and feelings.

On occasion patients who are brought to the first aid clinic, or worse still, the emergency department of a hospital, are too frightened to voice their needs, uncertainties or deep fears. The hospital ambience and queues are not conducive to their doing so. Actually, these two factors make patients feel quite unable to ask for any details which would clarify matters for them. Very often patients wait in total silence. Patients may realise that in all the prior confusion they might have forgotten to bring some money to pay for prescription charges, or even to buy themselves a drink. Some patients who do not have the moral courage or strength to speak openly express their emotions by crying or moaning. In such cases doctors should not limit themselves to answering questions: it is also their duty to understand what is truly prompting the tears and fears expressed. Often such emotional manifestations are just the tip of the iceberg. It is necessary for doctors to discover what is causing the anxiety. The patient is crying and afraid – why is this happening?

The priest Vincent Nagle, who aided the sick in a San Francisco hospital, wrote, in a book which is truly a testimony to his enormous humaneness, about one of his experiences: 'Rachel lay alone in a ward simply because there was nothing more which could be done to help her. Filled with despair she cried out constantly, and this was why she had been placed in an isolation ward. The doctors could not suppress her pain. Patients who reach the last stage of their illness where there is not much hope left are, sad to say, often placed in isolation. Nurses and doctors do not, in such cases, respond to their cries of pain. In general nurses are excellent and give freely of their care and dedication; they are usually prepared to do all they can to help. However, when this is not possible, they choose not to be available. This is caused by the fact that they feel uneasy.

'I heard a voice call out and made my way towards this cry of pain. I had no idea what I should do next, however a thought repeatedly flashed across my mind: "I must share this patient's suffering." I have always believed that Christ was also present and suffering *alongside* both of us. Christ did not ease the suffering of the man who was crucified at his right-hand side, nor that of the man on his left. He did nothing to lessen his Mother's pain or that of his Apostles. He just did not do so. On occasion we may all long for Christ to diminish our suffering; we soon learn, however, that he does not do this, because he loves us, and it is his wish that we live our mission in life to its fullest extent. Christ has never taken from any one of us the chance to fulfil our vocation.

'I entered the room and shut the door. Rachel was screaming. I fell to my knees and began to cry out, trying to drown her voice. I called out "Oh God, help her! Help her!" I hoped that my doing so would make her realise that she was not alone – someone else was praying with her. I spent many hours there. I do not know how long exactly and, at a certain point in time, I became aware that Rachel's blasphemies had turned to prayer. Her words were, "I offer You all my suffering. I beseech You to come to my aid". In the final moments of her life her despair had turned to hope.'[4]

The Dalai Lama reminds us: 'Our worst attributes are hatred, anger and being too attached to this world. It is our duty to acknowledge and recognise this and strive to lessen these negative forces within us. Love, compassion and awareness, on the other hand, are our best attributes, and we must do all possible to increase these positive forces.'

It is our sentiments and feelings that facilitate our ability to be of support to others. We must truly understand what we are feeling during different moments of our lives: when we are happy and exhilarated; when we are angry and discouraged; cheerful or depressed. We all go through a gamut of emotions, and it is our duty, as the Dalai Lama explained, to learn, after a period of profound thought, how to make proper use of them. We all possess innate qualities which allow us to deepen our self-awareness. These qualities also help us learn the correct way in which to relate to others. In the case of doctors, they learn, therefore, how to relate to their patients and begin to live solely for them.

There are times when professionals – such as doctors, nurses and carers – are totally immersed in their roles. They then discover that theirs is a difficult and onerous task, since their main objective is to act in the professional manner their roles demand. In hospitals those who wear white overalls or collars are easily identified as people having a certain authority, and, as such, appear both detached and unemotional. They seem taken up with promoting their image and careers and making sure they are treated with the decorum which their profession commands. They think only of themselves, forgetting the needs of the sick who surround them. It is at this point that patients believe they are lesser mortals, unworthy of attention.

Rogers has shown us which steps must be taken on these occasions: 'The safest method to use in order to solve basic problems and avoid acrimonious conflict is to openly, and without reservation, create valid relationships. In other words we must allow patients to give vent to their emotions in order for us to understand what is causing their feelings.'

Once we have listened to and understood the emotions expressed by our patients, we must then make an effort to reflect upon our interactions with them. Reflection (or reformulation) demands, as the psychologist Giulio Fontò, who participated for many years in our seminars on counselling, says, that we must stand before a mirror and examine our own feelings. Fontò points out: 'It is quite clear that family counsellors should openly show their emotions and not be distant or cold.'[5] In a certain way, and with some reservations, this also applies to health carers as they are often closely observed by the sick who, in turn, are in search of relevant details.

HOW TO RESPOND TO FEELINGS EXPRESSED BY PATIENTS

There are many different ways of reacting to sentiments expressed or questions asked. One may simply repeat or reflect what has been spoken by the other person. This would involve an answer which clearly reflects the doctor's understanding of a patient's fear. The answer may be brief, and may only involve a resumption of communication with the patient; giving importance to one or two important elements of his question in a clearly defined way. It would also involve highlighting the most important facts required. In this way doctors would show they have understood the patient well and are ready to give him or her the required importance.

Rogers points out that in this simple way each patient begins to feel that he is not alone. Neither is he being 'merely observed or scrutinised'. In other words, it is then possible to create a serene atmosphere in which a doctor-patient relationship based on trust can grow and mature.

In short, when doctors understand and accept the importance of openly expressing one's feelings, they are then able to give their patients greater help. It follows that:

1. The acceptance of our emotions is the key to a greater self-awareness, and the formation of relationships with others. Carl Rogers confirms: 'The intensity of my relationships with others is a result of the greater understanding of my own being, acquired through a deeper self-knowledge.'

2. Allowing patients to freely give voice to their emotions helps to put them at their ease. When speaking to doctors, patients should have the opportunity to speak about their suffering, pain, fear, anxiety and, if necessary, their depression.

3. When patients are allowed to express their sentiments they believe they are accepted unconditionally and are not being judged. The more a patient is listened to, the more he realises that he is being taken into consideration.

4. The expression of our sentiments facilitates communication with the sick and helps them understand that they are worthy of our consideration. What the patient puts into words is, for him, the truth.

5. A trusting relationship is created between doctors and patients when both parties express their emotions freely.

6. It is feelings that allow doctors not only to help their patients but also to give them both moral and physical support. It is then that together they can solve problems which arise.

Throughout the period of time when emotions are being expressed health-carers must, however, still adopt a professional stance and never give evidence of emotional involvement. It is certainly correct for them to share their patients' discomfort, but they must never allow themselves to become too emotionally involved.

Rogers' Ten Points

Carl Rogers' so-called ten points help doctors, nurses, psychologists, social workers and chaplains in their relations with patients. They are listed briefly hereunder:

1. Can I, being who I am, be perceived by the sick as being a person who deserves their confidence and is trustworthy and loyal in the true sense of the words?

2. Is it humanly possible for me to be sufficiently expressive so as to transmit to others in an unequivocal manner that I really am what I seem to be?

3. Am I at all capable of engaging with another person in a positive manner, offering warmth, care, interest and respect?

4. Am I sufficiently strong enough in character so as to be deeply respectful of my personal emotions and needs as I am of those of a sick person? Is it at all possible for me to express my emotions and needs, as if they were mine alone, and completely different from those of the sick person I am dealing with?

5. Am I self-confident enough to accept the fact that a patient may be totally different from me?

6. Is it possible for me to accept the sentiments and personal beliefs which are significant to the patient so completely as to make me quite unable to assess or judge him? Can I be sensitive enough to communicate fully with him without ever trampling on any of those beliefs which may be precious to him?

7. Am I prepared to accept every aspect of a sick person's character? Is it possible for me to accept him as he is? Am I able to show my total acceptance of him? Or is my acceptance only partial since I approve of some of his emotions but disapprove of others?

8. Is it possible for me to ensure that my patients will never face the threat of feeling that they are being judged?

9. Am I able to perceive in a patient a desire for change or am I limited by my perception of his and my own past?

10. Only a person who is psychologically mature can create a relationship in which the best possible help can be given to the sick. In other words, how I create a relationship which will allow others to mature and grow depends entirely on how psychologically mature I am myself.

ATTITUDES TO BE AVOIDED

If the above are the correct attitudes which must be adopted in order to create an ethical, dynamic rapport with patients, then there are others which must be avoided. The most common pitfall among doctors is their inability to understand how vital it is for them to be ready to listen attentively and with a sympathetic ear to all a patient needs to say. Both doctors and chaplains are all too often very keen on talking, but less ready to listen attentively to and empathise with their patients. To form a closer relationship with patients, the following attitudes are to be avoided at all costs:

- *Never be in too much of a hurry.* Patients need time to understand and absorb the information given to them by doctors.
- *Never be over-confident.* Doctors should never presume to believe they automatically have ready answers to patients' questions.
- *Never make hasty decisions.* Doctors need to take time to examine patients and also to listen to them prior to making decisions.
- *Never allow interruptions.* Nothing at all should ever be allowed to interrupt the dialogue between a doctor and his patient. This includes nurses walking in and out of the room and telephones or mobile phones ringing. Should this occur, it inevitably leads to a patient feeling he is not important enough to merit the doctor's full attention. At such moments patients believe they are being ignored.
- *Never lose a patient's trust.* Doctors should not, in any way, act in a manner which diminishes a patient's trust in them. Doctors must always respect the confidentiality, privacy and rights of each patient.

To summarise, all depends, as I have just pointed out, on a doctor's decision to be at a patient's disposal at all times. He must always be prepared to listen. Epictetus declared: 'God gave us one tongue and two ears. It follows, therefore that we should talk less and listen more.'

Umberto Veronesi affirms: 'Besides giving all their attention to patients, doctors must also respect their privacy. This, in turn, leads to yet another important factor which must always be kept in mind: a patient's right to confidentiality. It is thanks to the well-established law regarding doctor-patient confidentiality that the sick are guaranteed this. A doctor can never, even well-intentionally, violate a patient's privacy.' [6]

NOTES

1   AMCI (Associazione Medici Cattolici Italiani – Association of Italian Catholic Doctors), 3 October 1982.
2   E. Kübler Ross, *Death and Dying*, Cittadella Publishing, Assisi, 1979.
3   I.R. Marino, *Faith and Healing*, ed. Giulio Einaudi, Torino, 2005, pp. 82–3.
4   V. Nagle, *On the Frontier of the Human: A Priest Among the Sick*, Rubettino Publishing, Soveria Mannelli (CZ), 2004, p. 9.
5   Two-year formation course for family counsellors and social workers, Emigrant Family Centre, Berne, 1988–89, p. 11.
6   *A Caress for Healing: The New Medicine, A Balance of Science and Conscience*, Sperling & Kupfer, Milan, 2004, pp. 23–4.

CHAPTER 6

THE EIGHTH SACRAMENT: THE ABILITY TO LISTEN

I have always believed that patients benefit the most when they are listened to. Patients taken to an out-patients department to be examined by a doctor often feel anxious. If at that moment someone is readily available to listen to their needs however, the patients' fears subside. They begin to feel accepted and consoled. In today's technological world, the fact that hardly anyone is prepared to listen to others has become a scourge. This is especially so in patient-doctor relationships. All of us seem very keen to communicate in one way or another – via the telephone, mobile phone text messages and the internet, but professional relationships lack a human touch.

In October 2006 edition of the *Herald Tribune*, American author Jeremy Rifkin remarked: 'It seems that though communication is on the increase, people are saying less.' He added that college students are great at communication due to the fact that, on average, American children spend between five and six hours a day watching television and surfing the net. This, however, has caused them to be quite incapable of listening to those who surround them.

Doctors are also poor listeners. Situations have arisen wherein patients have felt both bitter and disillusioned. It is listening to one's patients that humanises medicine, just as man has humanised nature through his work (Marx). As Hans Jonas affirms: 'With reference to mankind, humanisation means no longer being subservient to nature and therefore having the opportunity to be oneself.' When doctors and nurses listen to a patient, they are showing recognition of that person's human dignity, making him the protagonist and a co-decider in the type of treatment they are proposing for him.

MEDICAL SCIENCE AND HUMANISTICS

The philosopher Hans Georg Gadamer wrote: 'Medicine in the West has reached its limits. It must now make radical changes and deepen its awareness of social behaviour.' Gadamer believes that modern science has transformed doctors into technicians capable of making a correct diagnosis, but only ready to enter a relationship with patients when these are admitted into hospital. Gadamer also says hospitals now resemble assembly lines. In essence he argues that medicine should once more become the 'art of healing', where communication between doctors and their patients is promoted.

When asked a question by the journalist Giancarlo Zizola, Don Luigi Verzè replied: 'It is enough to remember traditional medicine, from Hippocrates on, for us to understand the true value of the Hippocratic vision of health as the harmony of all the constituent elements of the human being: the soul, the psyche and the body … My vision is of a medical science which is at the centre of the human sciences and of life: the Athenian Health-Life. It would not be a revolutionary undertaking: Epidaurus and Alexandria were hospital-cities of life.'[1]

This has also been my own personal humanistic philosophy as well as the attitude I have adopted when dealing with the sick. As a consequence, listening has become an easy task. It has also meant that medicine is not only a means of curing patients, but has developed into a *sacred* art.

The sick find more comfort in a priest who listens than in one who merely spouts platitudes. I was in San Paolo, Brazil, when I first listened to Archbishop Cardinal Evaristo Arns, the Franciscan who backed the liberal theologian Boff with the Holy See when he spoke of the 'eighth sacrament'. Boff believed that listening was a sacrament through which the hearts and minds of people could be reached. Having previously been convinced by Carl Rogers' beliefs in a 'patient-centred therapy', I was made even more certain that listening empathetically was the best way to help people. The teaching and example of Cardinal Arns strengthened my beliefs and have made me the way I am. I greatly value my belief in the power of listening.

Monsignor Oscar Romero, the Archbishop of El Salvador, was assassinated in 1980. By nature a timid and conservative man, he had courageously spoken out after his friend, the Jesuit father Rutilio Grande, was gunned down and killed by a death squad. Monsignor Romero's actions impressed me. After his friend's assassination the Bishop took to listening to the poor peasants who went to him to speak of their suffering. They were penniless, desperate, and many among them were ill. The Bishop listened to them for hours on end. His was a paternal compassion. He began to have a clear picture of the injustice, violence and corruption which was rife in El Salvador. He then spoke out against the regime's wrong-doing, the actions of the military and the manner in which rich families behaved. The hours he spent listening to the peasants gave credence to his words. This led to his martyrdom.

Pope Paul VI, a man greatly disposed to listening to others, offers us yet another example. In the writing of his encyclical *Humanae vitae* he chose to listen to the voice of the Holy Spirit, rather than that of the Commission, set up by himself, to examine the problem of contraception. In his first encyclical *Ecclesiam suam* Pope Paul VI wrote: 'Prior to speaking, it is necessary for us to listen to the voice, or better still, the hearts of mankind. We must understand the needs of men and, as often as possible, respect them and when necessary, support them.' Cardinal Paul Poupard describes the Pope as being a man who listened and who was open to new ideas.[2]

The same rules apply to doctors and, if I may say so, to priests. During their formative training doctors are taught to make the correct diagnoses. The importance of listening to patients is, however, hardly mentioned.

Besides suffering physically, patients who long for comfort face uncertainty and unanswered questions which fill their minds and hearts. The sick, though acknowledging the initial symptoms of their illness, cannot understand what is wrong. They are filled with fear. They endeavour to assess what is happening to them, what it is that is causing the pain they feel, and very often they imagine a worst case scenario. Their illness is a mystery and all they can do is try to find answers to the many questions that assail them. After calling on their family doctor, patients are referred to specialists who advise that tests, such as CAT scans and MR scans, are to be taken. This only leads to an increase in their anguish and anxiety. They long to know what is happening. Very often, the answer they receive is, as the situation demands, rather vague: 'We must wait and see.' These words trigger despair. If, however, specialists took the time to speak to their patients, the latter would feel more at ease and, as such, would begin to have faith in the doctor. Doctors cannot acquire their patients' faith by merely acting in a professional way. A patient's sense of well-being is only created if he feels he has been listened to.

Sad to say, this did not occur when a dear friend of mine was diagnosed with pancreatic cancer. He was a young medical specialist full of life, an active member of a youth movement. It was difficult for him to accept this cruel twist of fate, and following what was a hardly reassuring conversation with a fellow doctor, he committed suicide. I would certainly not blame the doctor concerned, but that young man needed to talk to someone who would willingly listen to him.

LISTENING MAKES DOCTORS MORE HUMANE

Doctors become more humane when they learn to listen to their patients. The creation of a doctor-patient rapport requires time and attention to what is said and, very often, what is left unspoken by the patient. This goal can be reached if doctors begin to think of medicine as a vocation. Frequently a doctor's initial enthusiasm and ambition are soon forgotten – it is then that a doctor becomes merely one of many. Doctors must therefore constantly evaluate their attitudes and renew their commitment. Listening to patients helps doctors work with a renewed vigour and stops them thinking only of monetary compensation.

It would also help if doctors believed they must always be at the service of their fellow men. In this respect they then become doctor-priests. Doctors who practise their art as a manifestation of their love for God – and there are many such – are truly praiseworthy. As Cardinal Joseph Ratzinger wrote in *Servants of Your Joy*, our God is one who 'gladdens youth',[3] and 'fills the young with enthusiasm and courage'.[4]

Doctors must, at all times, be courageous and enthusiastic so as to transmit hope to patients undergoing medical examinations both in Out Patients' departments and in hospital wards.

In this regard I was impressed by Ignazio Marino's narration of his experience 'one night almost twenty-five years ago, when still a newly-fledged inexperienced doctor, on duty in hospital'. Marino is now a world-famous transplant surgeon, and I quote here directly from his writings: 'From a room in a surgical ward came loud cries of pain. An old diabetic patient, who was nearly blind, had had all his toes amputated. After the operation his fear made it impossible for him to fall asleep. As I walked past his door I felt there was nothing else I could do but enter the room, offer the patient a drink of water and then sit at the foot of his bed to await the arrival of a nurse to administer a sedative I had previously prescribed. The old man began to talk about himself, relating that as a young man he had been a fighter pilot during the First World War. He had flown a Spad XIII biplane, one of the best and most popular fighter planes of the time. The old patient recounted that during aerial battles the best tactic for escaping enemy fire was to take a sudden nose-dive and then immediately come back up on full-throttle in order to rapidly gain altitude. However, only the ablest of pilots could perform such manoeuvres without losing consciousness. The pilots' physical stamina and ability to overcome the sudden changes in pressure made the difference between life and death. He made references to the seemingly never-ending seconds in time when, though his vision was blurred, he still had to maintain control of the aircraft. He spent more than an hour relating this tale and I, in that time, learnt many facts which I would never have learnt from a history book. Like a man talking to his grandson, the old man, forgetting his fears, without having had any medication, was gradually overcome by tiredness and eventually fell asleep. He had, in reality, not been in need of a sedative. All he had needed was the company of another human being. During that hour-long conversation he had forgotten all his fears. I learned many things that night and, above all, a new lesson: Time is not money. Time given to patients is well-spent for it can prove to be therapeutic.'[5]

Marino quite rightly reaches the conclusion that 'time is not money'. Unfortunately a number of doctors believe it is their duty to keep to a time-table. There is nothing worse in a doctor-patient relationship (or in any other professional relationship) than a doctor who constantly calculates the time he is spending with each patient. Time-watching is not conducive to listening to patients. Doctors rush through visits because other people await their attention. This also means earning more money. Fortunately, many of the doctors I have met and worked with do not belong to this category of doctors.

EMPATHETIC LISTENING

Having a relationship with a patient has more to do with a loving understanding of that person than mere problem-solving. Doctors need to give their patients space and time, allowing them to express themselves freely. A doctor must understand a patient's feelings, thoughts and sufferings. When a patient realises that he has his doctor's uncompromising acceptance, he can begin to have faith in his doctor's ability and humanity. After this has taken place, a doctor-patient relationship can be established.

It is only after listening to their patients that doctors can begin to treat them not only medically, but holistically. Pope John Paul II, in the aforementioned address to Catholic doctors of 3 October 1982, said: 'In concrete terms one must declare that none of you can limit yourselves to being responsible for the treatment of organs or other parts of the body. All doctors must take on the treatment of each patient as a whole. Neither can it stop there. Doctors must furthermore involve themselves in interpersonal relationships which contribute to the patients' wellbeing.' Therefore listening authentically becomes a sacrament of love, acceptance and trust, fostering credibility in the professional side of the relationship.

Empathetic listening embraces both the sentiments and the emotions of each patient, which, as I have already pointed out, are merely the tip of the iceberg, beneath which are concealed the patient's world and his true personality. Consequently, before reacting to a patient's verbal outbursts or requests for help, doctors must identify what it is that the patient truly needs.

According to Carl Rogers, 'the safest way in which to discover the answers to fundamental questions and the deep conflict experienced by patients … is to learn precisely what the patient's spoken words actually mean'. A patient's conflicting or negative comments may arise from feelings of desperation. He may not have been given the correct treatment; he may have been examined by other doctors in different hospitals and consequently may have lost all hope of recovery. Instead of stifling or cutting short such outbursts, doctors should gently and gradually help each patient separate fact from fiction, at the same time offering him the assurance and trust he longs for.

In order to put my message across, I have often related a short story about a child called Pierino. Having been put to bed, the child asks his mother for a kiss and says he would like the lights to be left on. His mother leaves the room but Pierino soon calls out, 'Mum, I'm thirsty'. Fully aware of what is happening, Pierino's mother returns to her son's room with a glass of water. Pierino takes a little sip of the water, for he is not really thirsty. Once more he is kissed by his mother, after which he falls into a peaceful sleep. Clearly Pierino had not felt at all thirsty – he had merely longed for his mother to return to his room and she, understanding his need, had complied.

On occasion, patients are in need of a kind gesture which will encourage them to believe and hope that they can overcome their illness. Patients greatly appreciate a smile, a kind look, a warm handshake or a caress, as these kind deeds help put them at their ease and allay their fears. A scientific explanation or diagnosis of their illness does not have quite the same effect.

Empathetic listening lays the foundations for a good doctor-patient relationship. Patients who, on their first visit to a doctor or during their first medical examination in hospital, feel they have been understood, are content and during follow-up visits less anxious. A patient who is led to believe that a doctor has taken a personal interest in him no longer feels that he is merely another patient on the list, waiting to be examined. This is what Carl Rogers had become aware of when he wrote: 'Very early on in my work as a therapist I learned that simply listening to patients was a great source of comfort to them.'

Medical and nursing students must be instilled with a *listening culture* and encouraged to participate in *personal communication* with patients. It is enough to look at a patient's face and listen to him to understand his suffering, fear or loneliness. Students must also learn to interpret a patient's silence, since on occasion the sick are quite unable to express their sufferings and simply stare in silence. This is also a form of communication, no less expressive and moving for those who can interpret it.

LISTENING IS A SIGN OF LOVE

Listening empathetically allows a doctor to think of a patient not simply as another case of a particular illness, but as an individual manifestation of it i.e. they think of the patient suffering the illness, rather than of the illness in purely clinical terms. Patients learn to accept their fate and the suffering they may have to bear. If the doctor is a practising Christian, he should not neglect to exercise his charisma of 'doctor-priest' by making some small reflection on faith and hope in God's healing. Acting like a Christian in no way diminishes a doctor's professionalism. Very often patients crave Christian support, yet they rarely come across doctors who bear witness to Christ the healer in their daily rounds. Not only enlightened by scientific knowledge, but also inspired by the Holy Spirit, doctors and patients must work hand in hand to overcome an illness. Patients are deeply affected by their illnesses. They become physically fragile and weak. They feel inadequate and are unable to keep up with work, as they had done in the past. Being unable to bear pain, they ever so slowly lose the will to live. I have always taken to heart any questions or affirmations made to me by patients, especially cancer patients. I have been asked, 'Why am I still living?' or even, 'I cannot face the pain any more. I long to die'. These comments are understandably momentary outbursts, but there is often some truth in them.

Doctors who are present when a patient asks such questions or makes such declarations can help by simply listening and offering a kind gesture. This help becomes even more necessary when the patient concerned is struggling to overcome his illness, is troubled and in pain. In such situations, doctors, nurses and priests cannot do much else. The Sacrament of Anointing the sick not only fortifies patients but also has the power to heal. In a similar way, the eighth Sacrament of Listening is able to help patients resign themselves to their fate, filling them with hope and giving a sense to their suffering. Listening to patients is an act of love and at certain moments patients need to be loved, caressed and filled with fortitude. St Augustine's words have always been a great help: 'I do not understand how this occurs, but I do know that the suffering of any one person is lessened if others share his pain.'[6] Sharing a patient's suffering is an act of love, and love gives life.

Both God, in the Old Testament, and Christ, in the New Testament, give us clear proof of this reality. God listened to his people;[7] Christ listened to his flock,[8] to Nicodemus[9] and to the cry of the good thief.[10] Christ invites us to 'listen' to the parable of the sower of seeds and reminds us to 'Listen, anyone who has ears!'[11] Like a psychiatric therapist, the doctor needs to listen to himself and to the patient in order that he may meet all the needs of that person: the physical, the psychological and the spiritual.

The Bible refers to how God listens to us and has often spoken to mankind in general through individuals who were prophets. As Christ listened to the lamentations of a beggar, a widow, a paralysed man, a man born blind and to all those who do his will,[12] so much more should we who are doctors, psychologists, nurses, social workers, family counsellors and so on, listen empathetically, compassionately and with love to the words of all who approach us asking for help. Listening then becomes a mission in the lives of those who work with the sick, the marginalised, drug addicts and the needy. The Blessed Mother Teresa of Calcutta and many others like her listened and offered their services to the needy. Indeed their lives were devoted to caring for others.

It is an essential premise of the initial doctor-patient relationship that the patient should be regarded as a 'brother' to be listened to; then doctors may go on to verify what is wrong, carry out tests, reach a diagnosis, decide on a course of treatment and work towards a cure. A sense of brotherhood is the basis of faith and science. In the eyes of God, who sees beyond any incidental morphological and mental differences, all the sick are equal, as they should be also in our eyes, without discrimination between rich and poor: those who can afford private healthcare and those who must rely on public health services. Whichever the type of hospital, public or private, its primary care should be to put the human person in all his dignity and his irrefutable rights at the centre of its mission. This is what I was immediately aware of when I first came to the San Raffaele, this temple of medicine and suffering, where the driving force was the belief in the goodness of God: 'God is good – God loves mankind – God does not want Death, for he is life – God has commanded us to: go forth, teach and heal.' This is what makes the practice of medicine a priesthood, which administers 'God's medicine' (Rafel).

Enzo Bianchi, the Prior of Bosé Monastery, says the following about the importance of listening in his book, *I Was A Stranger and You Welcomed Me*: 'Having greeted your guest, invited him in and asked him to make himself at home, it is then necessary for you to listen to him: you must, before listening to his words, listen to his "presence", try to understand what his needs are. Listening involves giving up your time for him, allowing him to speak ... a stranger is no longer a stranger when we listen to what he says ... Listening, in actual fact, means keeping silent so as to give importance and trust to whatever others say ... *When we listen to others, we make them a part of ourselves*, we welcome them, understand them and make space for them in ourselves.'[13] The same may be said of our relationships with the sick.

Since listening is a sign of solidarity and love which is part and parcel of the holistic care of a person, it should be accompanied by tangible gestures of love during our accompaniment of the sick through his illness. The best conclusion for this chapter about the eighth sacrament was written by my friend, the journalist Emilio Bonicelli, whose life was suddenly devastated by illness, in his book *A Return to Life*: 'Throughout my days of suffering, by way of the company of friends who stood by me, and assisted by the prayers of all who supported me, a supreme Being gave answers to all my doubts.'[14]

NOTES

1   G. Zizola, *A Wing for Healing*, San Paolo, Cinisello Balsamo (MI), 1997, p. 176.
2   *Jesus*, August 1983, pp. 59–62.
3   Ps 42:4.
4   J. Ratzinger, *Ministers of Your Joy*, Àncora, Milano, 2002.
5   I.R. Marino, *Believing and Healing*, Giulio Einaudi Publishing, Torino, 2005, pp. 80–1.
6   Saint Augustine, Epistle 99:2.
7   Ex 23:21; Deut 4:30; 4:36.
8   Jn 10:3.
9   Jn 3.
10 Lk 23:39-43.
11 Mt 13:9.
12 Rizzoli, Milano, 2006, pp. 96–8.
13 E. Bonicelli, *A Return to Life: The Story of a Man's Battle with Leukaemia*, Jaca Books, Milan, 2002, p. 142.

Chapter 7

The pastoral care of the sick

I had gone to a large hospital in Lombardy to visit a friend. His wife had called me on the phone to say that his unsuccessful fight against cancer was almost over, so I had dropped everything and gone to visit him. His wife was in the hospital room with him when I arrived. On seeing him, I could tell the end was near and asked his wife if he had been given the sacrament of the sick. 'No,' she replied, 'and when the priest passed by yesterday, he was already in this state.'

We called the old chaplain who brought the holy oil with him and told me that the lady had not asked for her husband to have the sacrament administered the previous day, so he had left without asking whether he should administer it.

I think the above episode needs no further comment; the hospital chaplain nowadays has a much broader pastoral mission than simply that of administering sacraments to the sick.

Nowadays people normally go to hospital not to die, but to get well. I have seen countless patients urgently brought in on stretchers or being resuscitated, who later left on their own two feet. Patients no longer undergo long stays in hospital: even heart patients leave only a few days after an operation. I was surprised by a bishop's comment when he said: 'Nowadays the chaplain does not have much to do in hospital: people only stay a few days.'

But it is precisely *because* hospital stays are so short that the chaplain's mission is more necessary than ever. In a large hospital especially, just one chaplain working alone has no time to talk to and build up a spiritual relationship with patients. The first couple of days of a patient's stay are taken up with clinical tests, and then, perhaps by the third day, the chaplain might have occasion to visit and talk to the patient.

Around 40 per cent of the annual seventy-three thousand patients who stay at the Milan San Raffaele are alienated from the Church and the sacraments. Despite this fact, it is only a very small percentage of patients who will refuse human contact with the chaplain. Over the years I have witnessed conversions and 'rebirths' in the Holy Spirit.

PASTORAL COUNSELLING AND THE HOSPITAL

A secularised, hectic and technologically-imbued modern culture, in which medical practice has been emancipated from religious values and from all that was once held sacred pervading even hospitals of Catholic inspiration, leaves no room for the traditional figure of the chaplain. In today's context, the chaplain is an endangered species: he is out of place and risks marginalisation. His services, despite being accepted on paper, have become superfluous and marginal to health management, to the doctors and ward sisters. This is all the more evident in public hospitals, where the secular environment tends to be even less welcoming of the presence of a priest than in Catholic-run hospitals.

I have often been irked by the way heads of Catholic hospitals always have words of praise for the scientists, researchers and doctors, only rarely for the nursing staff, and none at all for the chaplaincy team who are at the service of patients twenty-four hours a day. Such an unfair elitist attitude causes disappointment.

So the evangelical command to 'Go out, teach and heal'[1] becomes almost impracticable. Once this Pentecostal command of the Church falls by the wayside, the very essence of its spiritual mission of teaching, healing and sanctifying comes into question. This is not merely a threat but a fact which may already be noted, despite the innovative action taken after Vatican II. It is therefore necessary to receive the message, the doctrine and the developments following the Second Vatican Council and to put them into action in a tangible way that gives credibility to the Church and its mission.

This is not simply a question of bringing oneself up to date for the sake of being up to date, which a pastor or any Christian can do.

It is also a binding responsibility and a duty, for what is at stake here is the essence of Christianity in a society that has changed completely. The present cultural context in the field of healthcare calls for a renewed Christian presence. The Italian Bishops' Conference Report stresses that the available tools which must be put to use are the pastoral council and the hospital chaplaincy. The first of these is responsible for programming and coordination; the second is responsible for evangelisation, catechesis and the administration of the sacraments.

We must admit that such tools make possible the transition from the kind of pastoral care that is unproductive, serving to disperse rather than unify, one-dimensional and passive, to a pastoral care that is dynamic, living, multidimensional, and that brings about the active involvement of Christians who are engaged in helping the suffering. This could bring to light a new ecclesiasticism based on Vatican II, which is an ecclesiasticism of participation founded on the common priesthood of the people, received in baptism.

The Church envisioned by Vatican II is not based on the old paternalistic clerical-lay distinction, but is one in which all are united as a responsible, mature people of God, enriched by their diversity and the many charisms endowed by the Holy Spirit for the co-responsible edification of God's kingdom. To enable this, the above-mentioned institutions (pastoral council and hospital chaplaincy) will only be faithful manifestations of the Church if the Church itself is represented in them by a plurality of charisms (presbyters, deacons, religious and lay people) as a united people of God.

According to past experiences, the hospital chaplaincy chronologically precedes and prepares the way for the pastoral council. But in order to do this properly, the chaplaincy itself – as an autonomous parish – should clarify its own structure as well as its mission. As a manifestation of religious service rendered to the Christian communities in hospitals, the hospital chaplaincy should be made up of at least one or two priests, and a deacon, a religious sister and lay people. Its principal objectives are:

- To be a clear sign of the presence of the Church in each hospital by having readily approachable representatives of the Church who can carry out its mission.
- By means of the members of the chaplaincy team, by their attitude and deeds, including the administration of the sacraments, to provide a revelation of God's love for mankind and his closeness in times of distress, helping sufferers to the very end.
- To promote and coordinate the various strengths of the hospital community by means of the appropriate tools and initiatives – and this is where the pastoral council occupies a central role.
- To involve all Christians present on the premises in the promotion of good health and in the care of the sick.

The chaplaincy team provides a pastoral care which responds to the needs of today. Mainly centred on humanisation and evangelisation, it is work which requires not only greater 'professionalism' on the part of the chaplain, but a diversification of approaches, of charisms and abilities, by involving all of its members, rather than relying on the single ability of the one priest. This model of a chaplaincy does away with the dangerously 'boring' old-fashioned idea of the Church, still at large today, in which the many duties of the chaplain (evangelisation, catechesis and the administration of the sacraments) are reduced to just the administration of the sacraments.

The sacraments, which are visible signs of grace strengthening faith, need to be preceded and prepared for by evangelisation and an adequate catechesis actualised by humane caring for and help of patients, so that the symbols of God's love for humanity are not separated from the actuality and immediacy of that love.

Without this, the Faith is in danger of seeming very shallow and superficial, contributing nothing to God's people's greater knowledge of him, but on the contrary leading to a greater ignorance of God, and the sacraments which are signs of his love. The best traditions confirm the fact that the Church has never been in a hurry to confer the sacraments; on the contrary, they are the point of arrival, the climax reached through a responsible preparation which makes the patient a new and responsible member of the Church i.e. one of God's people making up the Church.

CHRIST'S PRESENCE AMONG THE SICK

The mission of the chaplain and the chaplaincy is founded on the presence of Jesus Christ in the sick, or rather, on an identification of the sick with Christ, for the good which may be done to them.[2] From his Incarnation to his Passion, Christ lived and suffered for them, like them and with them: *Jesus, Deus Patiens* (Jesus, the suffering God). The sick are therefore a revelation of the suffering Christ; tabernacles of the Son of God made man.

The mystery of the Incarnation is at the centre of the sacramental and pastoral life of a hospital. As defined by that excellent medic Clemente Alessandrino, Christ is incarnated in the suffering of every sick person. The model for the chaplaincy and the hospital is Jesus Christ, God made man. 'The wondering crowds exult'[3] and 'glorify him together with the God who sent him':[4] this is what happened when Christ was among us.

God lives in every sick person: in the newborn as well as the patient battling cancer. Christ is incarnate in each human being, because God said, 'I have made man in my image and likeness'.[5] 'Christ is God's love made flesh,' wrote Pope Benedict XVI in his first encyclical *Deus Caritas est*: 'Christ identifies with the needy: the hungry; the thirsty; strangers; the poor; the sick; prisoners. "Whenever you do this to the least of my brothers, you do it unto me."[6] Love of God and love of one's neighbour go hand in hand: in the littlest person we meet Christ and in Christ we meet God.'[7]

Christ, who spoke the words, 'All that you do for one of these little ones, you do it for me', is to this day a healer of the sick. Christ gives life. To the leper, who said to him: 'Lord, if it is your will, I can be cured', what was Jesus' reply? 'It is my will: you are cured.'[8] Christ's love and compassion heal mankind, for they take away all that is evil, and man grows closer to being God's image: *imago Dei*. God created mankind not to sickness, but to a full life. The scriptures remind us that 'God did not create death. He made all things that they may live.' It has been rightly said that sickness has no substance, what exists is the sick person, in both body and soul.

The priest who carries out the ministry of chaplain is Christ's witness before the patients and all the hospital staff. He must see 'the face of Christ' in himself and in the sick. In such a way, his work becomes truly a sacred ministry.

In the words of the Pope, the chaplain is like the 'good servant of Jesus Christ, always in action' compelled by his 'love for Christ'.[9] In Benedict XVI's encyclical we may perceive the outline of the 'worker of charity' and the 'ministry' of the chaplain. Addressing those helpers of the bishops who carry out the practical charitable work of the Church, he exhorts them to be 'guided by the faith which is made practical through love.[10] They need, therefore, to be people motivated by a love for Christ, people whose hearts Christ has won with his love, so awakening their love for their neighbour'.[11]

THE PRIEST'S EVANGELISING ROLE IN HOSPITALS

A priest should be someone who makes the effort to get to know the patient's way of thinking and background, and who can understand his or her suffering. Without a strong motivation of love, charity, solidarity, desire to be helpful and spirituality, he cannot evangelise, nor can he humanise.

The priest should be sought after by both doctors and patients and should always be available to all, giving the whole of his being. He should not, as sometimes happens, clock in at work and leave after a short while because his services are not required. In a place where people are working together night and day, there should always be an available chaplain on duty. For this reason he must be free to go to patients whenever called. He must be an expert in human relations and become the focal point of the hospital.

I was struck by the words of Professor Guido Pozza, a friend of mine, and a mainstay of the San Raffaele since 1972, when he said: 'A doctor, like a priest, should feel the need to follow up his patients, and after that, if a friendly and comfortable relationship develops, it will enable him to guide the patient along the road to physical and emotional recovery and health in line with Kantian philosophy, which places the person at the centre of our work.'[12] These words apply to both doctors and priests, who both accompany the patient in suffering and (should) collaborate in his spiritual and physical recovery. The passage from Hippocrates, 'I will enter any house, and I shall go there in order to relieve the sick' may apply to both doctor and priest.

The difference between a doctor and a priest is in the fact that the priest's ministry is evangelisation, but this does not exclude a Christian doctor from evangelising, prudently, during the execution of his professional duties. Christ's exhortation to 'Go out, teach and heal' is for all Christians. In the evangelical vision, both the doctor and the priest are Christ's apostles and therefore both are Christ's priests by whose means he may come and heal the sick.

The motto of the Neapolitan St Giuseppe Moscati, himself a medical doctor, was: 'Science alone is insufficient to change the world; to do this we must act honestly and lovingly.' He was an evangeliser, a true doctor-priest among the sick, especially among the poor and those whose suffering was greatest during the cholera epidemic. He considered his profession a vocation: a mission to serve God through his suffering brothers and sisters by relieving their suffering as much as he could, doing his utmost with great love for all who were sick. He is a just model for our times, both for priests and for doctors to follow.

Benedict XVI affirms that through the centuries 'with the passage of time and the spread of Catholicism, the exercise of charity: showing love for the widowed and the orphaned, prisoners, the sick and the poor … became a confirmed and essential role of the Church, along with the administration of the sacraments and the spreading of the Word'.[13]

Nowadays, younger priests especially, unless they are hospital chaplains, are not in as close contact with the sick as used to be the case when a parish priest carried the Blessed Sacrament to the sick in their homes or in hospital. This mission has been delegated to lay Eucharistic ministers, the priest only visiting occasionally to hear confession. A lack of vocations and pastoral preparation for ministry among the sick are part of the reason for this. However, in any pastoral programme the sick should be the first to receive Christ and his Word, the Eucharist and Love, rather than the last.

A TYPICAL DAY IN THE LIFE OF A CHAPLAIN

The hospital chaplain's day is an extremely busy one and his constant presence and availability are required in order that he may participate in the salvific mission of Christ in the healing of the sick. He is not there merely to be a 'presence' but is the focal point, the dynamo which brings Christ's mission to life for those who are suffering. He is called to heal the sick in body and soul, as Christ did. 'Go, your faith has cured you.'[14] When he absolves the sins of the patient with the words of Christ, he says, 'Go, and sin no more'.[15]

The chaplain's dealings with the sick and with hospital personnel should be informed by an ethic which may best be described as 'bioethics in the tradition of the Beatitudes', as Salvino Leone teaches in his fine work, *The Theological Perspective in Bioethics*.[16] Among the new ethical 'horizons' he proposes four fundamental possibilities, referring to them in the words of the psalmist: medicine with a humble heart; doctors of generous spirit; patients of sound spirit; a society which follows the path of justice. These 'beatitudes' must be deeply rooted in the heart, and in the manner with which the chaplain carries out his duties.

The most significant moment for the chaplain is the celebration of the Eucharist, often in the presence of patients, their relatives and hospital staff. Christ gives himself as the bread of life to 'heal' the sick. In the aforementioned encyclical, Pope Benedict XVI writes: 'The *Logos* – the Word – has truly become food for us – like love. The Eucharist makes us party to the sacrificial act of Christ. We do not receive the incarnate Word in a passive way, but we become involved in the action of the offering.'[17] From the hospital chapel Christ is carried to the sick by priests, nuns and Eucharistic ministers.

The idea of transmitting Holy Mass over the radio or closed circuit TV to all hospital rooms is a good one. It was something I experienced at the Columbus clinic near the Fiera in Milan, run by the Missionary Sisters of the Sacred Heart, founded by St Francesca Cabrini. If the patient so wishes, he may follow Holy Mass or other religious functions which are taking place in the chapel. The camera focuses on the altar, the tabernacle, the crucifix and the Madonna. It is not uncommon for patients to keep their TV sets on through the night in order to feel close to Christ in the tabernacle even though he is already, in fact, present in their suffering.

Just as doctors do their rounds of the wards during the day, so should the hospital chaplain, meeting the sick, their families and the hospital workers at the bedside. Visiting the sick is one of the works of Charity; in each patient the priest meets Christ, for the patient is the embodiment of the suffering Christ. The Jewish verb for 'visit' is 'to see', and 'to see implies appreciation, consideration, providence, knowledge. To be visited therefore means to be appreciated and so respected and esteemed, being significant to someone'.[18] When the chaplain stands at the sick person's bedside, it is almost as though he is standing at 'God's altar', because the rite of suffering of the Passion and Resurrection of Christ is being celebrated on that bed. The priest-patient relationship during these visits is a testimony to the love and solidarity of the spirit of a priest and a shepherd.

Visits to the sick should not consist of a brief greeting followed by a quick exit from the patients' rooms or ward. Together with various chaplains, I have always assessed the quality and content of visits. It is true that the chaplain would like to visit all the patients in the wards assigned to him, but this should not be done at the cost of the quality of visits. The patient needs to be listened to, and to converse, because solitude often leads to feelings of abandonment and distrust. The patient needs to communicate: to talk about his or her sickness and, moreover, to express his or her feelings.

The Book of Job[19] expresses the feelings of the sick man when his 'brothers' and 'friends' stay away from him. He does not even see his 'neighbours and acquaintances' any longer and therefore he feels like a 'stranger' and a 'foreigner'. He is even denied by his own wife and children, and those he once loved have turned against him. This passage from the Book of Job sounds exaggerated, but is true of some situations in which patients suffer acute illnesses.

I felt I had recognised Job in one young man of twenty-five. Stefano was in hospital with AIDS following a long and tortured history of drug abuse, short stays in rehabilitation centres and, when still a minor, some months in a reformatory. He had fought his illness alone for years, and it had by this stage reduced him to a state similar to Job's. He had lost contact with his parents who, after many years of sacrifice and attempts to help him, had finally thrown him out. He was alone and lived, with a group of homeless people, close to the train station and a community centre. In his last year of life he had made a slight recovery, but his true miracle was his meeting with Christ, whom he grew to love and long for in the Eucharist, and who became his only consolation. He felt ostracised, just like the leper in the Gospel,[20] but, like the leper (to many, AIDS is, unfortunately, just like leprosy), he met Christ, and after so many years he suddenly fell in love with him. What he ardently desired was to have someone listen to the story of his conversion rather than someone to console him.

When he was about to be released from hospital he was desperate to speak to his parents and ask their forgiveness. He longed to be with his brothers and sisters and, like the prodigal son, run into his father's arms. He had not seen his father since he was twenty-one. Learning of this, I offered to call his parents, whom he had described as 'church-goers'. We prayed together before the phone call, and I made the call in his presence. A soft-spoken female voice answered the call, but the tone sharpened as soon as I mentioned Stefano's name: 'Absolutely not. Stefano is dead to us', and the receiver was replaced without another word. I blanched, and Stefano let out a cry of anguish, saying: 'Now I feel truly abandoned by all, apart from yourself and Christ.' A year later, Stefano made a holy death and joyfully went to his Father's heavenly home. And today, the mother, who had never gone to visit and listen to her sick son, now visits his grave and talks to him every week.

This event, like many others, has left an indelible impression on my heart, so that whenever I visit a sick person, I feel more human. And this involves making room for the patient, for he or she is the master. The sickbed is a place of enlightenment because I find the resignation of the patient edifying. When I find that I am not welcomed by a patient because that person is bitter and angry with God, I accept this as a humbling of myself and return to try again another time. Often I am welcomed on the second visit, and the patient is eager to explain his earlier reluctance to see me. The shepherd must never abandon the lost sheep.

VISITS TO THE SICK

Ethical behaviour in relation to patients demands of the chaplain, whether of a public or a Catholic hospital, a certain mode of presentation and attitude. Below are a few words of advice worth considering when one is visiting patients, especially for the first time:

1.   Apart from some form of religious sign like a cross and a collar, the chaplain should wear an identity tag clearly showing his name and role in the hospital.
2.   Visits should be timed for when the patient is free from doctors' rounds or examinations.
3.   In order to give the patient privacy, it is preferable if the chaplain's visits do not coincide with those of family and friends. If the patient asks to be heard in confession or would like to talk in confidence, anyone else who happens to be present should be politely asked to leave the room for a while.
4.   The chaplain is concerned with the sick person and not with the illness, so questions about the illness and its causes should be completely avoided.
5.   Any talk regarding the patient's illness, treatment, therapy or any complaints about the way the hospital is run should be absolutely avoided. If a patient confides such problems the chaplain should suggest he speak to the head nurse or ward sister or somebody else responsible for such things, like the public relations officer or a social worker.

6.   The chaplain should stick to the true purpose of his visit, which is to create a rapport between himself and the patient on a spiritual and pastoral level, as a minister of the Word and the sacraments.

7.   It is always hard to begin conversation. One could break the ice by making some general and neutral, but empathetic statement.

8.   The chaplain should demonstrate his willingness to listen to the patient with empathy and give him or her all the time he or she needs. Often patients will confide their history and seek to personalise their illness. It must not be forgotten that before being a patient, this is a person, often with a family history.

9.   The patient always has something to talk about – this is a human characteristic. However, at times he or she will go silent in the presence of the chaplain and might simply nod or perhaps make a complaint, or grumble about the doctors. In such situations it is best to let him talk rather than attempt to defend the hospital. Often this is merely a letting-off of steam rather than a real complaint.

10. The chaplain should also allow for non-verbal communication. Often, one can discern the personality and the sufferings of a person simply from facial expressions and the positioning of the person's body. In that face and suffering body is Christ incarnate.

11. The most important phase of the visit or the relationship between the chaplain and the patient is when one is attempting to enter a communion of faith, charity and hope with the patient by means of the Church represented by the chaplain. It is a moment of great grace, in which the patient is the suffering Christ – *Jesus Patiens*. The biblical scholar Luciano Manicardi of the Bosé community writes: 'St Matthew's words: "I was sick and you visited me" may be turned to "Christ visits us in the sick". He who visits the sick may discover that he himself is being visited by Christ in the sick person.'

12.   The chaplain should diplomatically make known his availability to administer the sacraments – Holy Communion, Confession and the Sacrament of the Sick – should these be needed or desired. If the patient is mobile and can leave his bed, the chaplain may explain the way to the closest church or chapel and give information on – perhaps even leave a leaflet detailing – schedules for available religious services like Holy Mass and recitation of the rosary.

13.   If a patient is due to be operated on for some serious condition, the chaplain may invite him to receive the Sacrament of the Sick, explaining that this is nowadays considered an aid to recovery rather than 'Extreme Unction', so that neither the patient nor his family become unduly alarmed by the offer.

14.   Before leaving the patient, on this first visit, the chaplain might give him some small religious token such as rosary beads, a miraculous medal of the Madonna, a crucifix or a picture of the Madonna of Life (the emblem of the San Raffaele). It has been rare for such gifts to be refused. It goes without saying that such a gift should not be offered to any patient who professes a lack of faith (although such patients will often accept such a gift anyway, to pass it on to a husband/wife/mother) or to those who are not Catholic or Christian. Such religious tokens are normally greatly welcomed by patients in public hospitals, where there are no religious symbols in any of the rooms or wards. The patients appreciate having them and place them on their bedside tables, in plain public view.

THE ADMINISTERING OF THE HOLY EUCHARIST TO PATIENTS

While I was laid up in hospital for over two months following an accident in which I had been hit by a car in Milan (while standing at a pedestrian crossing waiting for the lights to turn green), I had the opportunity to observe the way some priests and lay ministers administer the Eucharist to the sick.

Many patients wish to receive Holy Communion daily and very often choose to stay in hospitals where spiritual guidance is guaranteed on a regular basis. To be honest, so far there is no dearth of this, even in public hospitals; however, where it is not available, patients can only receive communion on Sundays.

Voluntary religious workers could inform patients of the available services and let the chaplain know which patients would like to receive Communion and who would like to be heard in confession before that. The adequate preparation and formation of volunteer lay Eucharistic ministers is a must: these should be fit for the office and be appointed by the Curia.

The Eucharist is nowadays carried to patients in a discreet manner; in the past, the chaplain would be accompanied by a couple of nuns carrying torches and ringing a hand bell to warn anybody in his path to act reverently. I remember this happening when I was a student in Rome and had to spend some time as a patient in the hospital run by the Irish 'Blue Sisters' close to Santo Stefano Rotondo. This very public display of the carrying of the Holy Eucharist to the sick is still practised in some hospitals I have visited outside Europe, though perhaps with less pomp and ceremony. In some hospitals the chaplain will wear a white stole, announcing the presence of the Eucharist to hospital staff he might meet along the way, so that they may behave with due decorum and respect. Each chaplain may have his own way of administering Holy Communion, as long as it is according to the rites of the Holy Church. It is important to choose a time that is convenient for the patient, and one should consult the ward sister in order to ensure that the patient will indeed be in the room and free to participate at the stipulated time.

It often happens, especially before patients are about to undergo a major operation, that they ask to be given Communion, but their situation in life does not permit the chaplain's acquiescence, for example, in situations where they are separated or divorced from their spouses, or cohabiting with somebody to whom they are unmarried. In such cases the chaplain must gently explain that this is not permissible. *Familiaris consortio* recommends: 'An even more generous, intelligent and prudent pastoral commitment, on the example of the Good Shepherd, is needed in dealing with families who, often through no fault of their own, or through circumstances not of their own making, find themselves in difficult situations.'[21]

Such irregular situations are dealt with in *Familiaris consortio*[22] and recommendations for pastoral action are made. The first to be discussed are 'pastors who, for love of truth, are obliged to discern situations accurately'. The discernment of such difficult cases in hospital through fifty years of counselling has caused me to share a great deal of suffering in empathy with people in irregular relationships who desired to receive the Lord in Holy Communion before undergoing an operation, say, or while the chaplain accompanied them during the terminal phases of their illness, in attempting to practise that same compassion which Christ felt for sinners. The *Catechism of the Catholic Church* teaches that 'the dying have the right to live their last hours with dignity and above all with the support of prayer and the sacraments in preparation for their meeting with the risen Christ'.[23] At such moments reconciliation with God and union with Christ in the Eucharist is what the patient needs from the Church, represented by the chaplain.

THE GOSPEL OF SUFFERING

In his apostolic epistle *Salvifici doloris*, John Paul II invites us to reflect on a profound teaching in the section which deals with the Gospel of Suffering. The following points are a summary of the Pope's words (25):

- At Christ's side, in the first and most elevated position, is his Holy Mother, whose whole life serves as a prime example of the Gospel of suffering.
- With her *presence* and *compassion*, Holy Mary offered a particular contribution to the Gospel of Suffering.
- Christ did not hide the necessity of suffering from his listeners: 'If anyone wants to be a follower of mine, let him renounce himself and take up his cross every day and follow me.'[24]

- At various points, the Gospel of Suffering talks of suffering 'for Christ' and 'because of Christ'.
- It has been observed over the centuries that a special strength is inherent in suffering, a special grace which brings men close to Christ. The Pope reminds us that many profound saintly conversions have been brought about through this grace. Two examples of such converts are St Francis of Assisi and St Ignatius Loyola. Suffering brings about a deep inner transformation: the meeting with Christ is conversion.

For each one of the Pope's reflections I can cite true examples of the Gospel of Suffering lived by my patients, who evangelised me and all those who worked around their sickbeds, especially doctors and nurses, who were struck by the great faith of their patients, despite the fact that perhaps – as the Pope states – 'each person endures suffering with the typically human protestation "Why?"[25] It is Christ, with his own suffering and passion on the Cross, who answers the question "Why?"'

One example of such a patient was Anna, who travelled in hope from Sicily to Milan to be operated on for a brain tumour. She accepted her fate and when she cried, it was only for her husband who was filled with doubts and anger and lacked faith. Her suffering purified her husband, bringing him to join her in accepting her illness. This wife and mother had a supernatural strength because she relinquished her struggles, letting herself go in Christ's arms, leaving her fate in his hands and in those of the Madonna of Lourdes, having been a voluntary helper of the sick pilgrims to that shrine. Her husband, who had always before been a distanced observer of her voluntary work, having been immersed in his own work, has now, through her suffering, found 'the divine strength' which has purified his natural 'human weakness'.

Suffering purifies the sick and is never a 'waste', for it is channelled into a spring of clear water from which those who are distanced from the faith may drink and be converted. The Pope teaches us that 'the Church feels the need to turn to the value of human suffering in the salvation of the world'.

A well-known intellectual who had a pancreatic tumour spent some weeks in the hospital, where many of his intellectual friends, acquaintances and a number of journalists would come to visit him. He enjoyed these visits, even if some were only made out of a sense of duty on the part of the visitors, but he was happiest when avidly listening to two of his fellow patients talking about their lives, families, work and faith. These two were neither intellectuals nor professionals: one was a labourer, the other a farmer from Calabria, but they were both filled with the Holy Spirit. Simply, and with great faith, they tried to help me pray for their 'sick brother'. They would offer up Holy Communion and their own suffering for his needs. Their devotion brought about a crisis of faith in their intellectual fellow patient, who would beg me to help him to believe in God, with tears in his eyes. He said over and over: 'I so much wish to have faith, like my friends here, but I do not know how to pray after having lived as an agnostic for forty years.' After some weeks of watching them pray, he self-consciously managed to mumble the name of Jesus under his breath. I reassured him that he was hungry for Christ, and because he truly did desire to have faith, in the end he was hugging and kissing the cross of St Benedict. The two 'Samaritans' were granted the consolation of evangelising their intellectual friend before they died; this happened in part due to his own suffering, and thanks to their testimony, despite the fact that they humbly said that they were 'as simple as the Apostles had been'. During my funeral homily for the intellectual, with the permission of his wife and children, I was allowed the grace of narrating the story of this conversion, which was the fruit of suffering. Among the mourners were many unbelievers, but I think (from feedback I have had, and from what I've read in the newspapers) that it was a lesson on life and that the 'teachers' were two 'simple' travelling companions along the road to eternity.

THE SACRAMENT OF THE SICK

What profoundly consoled my intellectual friend had been the administration of the sacrament of the sick to his two 'brothers'. He had cried, and I had not hesitated in anointing him too with the holy oil.

Christ instituted this seventh sacrament 'especially for the purpose of comforting those who are being tested by sickness'.[26] Like the Holy Eucharist, it is a sacrament of love, for it is Christ who heals body and soul. In James' Epistle is contained the following fundamental thought: 'If one of you is ill, he should send for the elders of the church, and they must anoint him with oil in the name of the Lord and pray over him. The prayer of faith will save the sick man and the Lord will raise him up again; and if he has committed any sins, he will be forgiven.'[27] The reading of this text to the sick before the administration of the sacrament calls for a brief reflection on their lives.

In the administration of the sacrament of the sick, the Church prays, together with the patient and those around him, for his salvation, reconciliation, healing and the forgiveness of his sins. For this reason the sacrament should be administered when the patient is conscious, and with mental faculties intact, therefore able to understand what is taking place, rather than at the very end of his life. The taboo attached to this sacrament by the family, as a result of popular culture and religious ignorance born of a lack of proper catechesis, should not exist. It is true that this sacrament was called 'Extreme Unction' in the past; this was because it used to be administered to people on their deathbeds. However, it is in fact a sacrament which supports, helps and gives hope to the sick, so much so that it is administered once or twice a month to those in hospital as well as out patients in many hospital chapels. This also gives new impetus to a more meaningful way of administering the sacrament to affect the Christian community, as it is a great treasure for the Church and for the sick. Each one of us is, to a greater or lesser extent, a potential patient, for even if we have no physical ailments, we all carry some wound to the heart that needs healing.

Sr Briege McKenna, an Irish nun, was crippled by an attack of rheumatoid arthritis while working in Florida. One day, during the Eucharistic Celebration, the Lord commanded her to get off her wheelchair, saying: 'I need you Briege. Stand up and walk.' Some time later, she received the charisma of healing from the Holy Spirit, and is now well known all over the world. In Italy she is known by the charismatic groups of Rimini and Rome. Her book *Miracles Do Happen* is truly wonderful and a means of evangelisation which touches the most indifferent of hearts, as I have learnt from a number of patients and doctors.

On the subject of the Sacrament of the Sick she writes: 'It is a great pity that so many who receive the Sacrament of the Sick do not truly expect healing. This is not a sacrament for the dying. It is for the living. It is for life: it brings healing on all levels. All one needs is a faith that is more alive.'[28]

It is true that this is a part of pastoral work, but the doctors and nurses who practise a personalised ethic cannot possibly be ignorant of the effectiveness of this sacrament in healing, even if they themselves are unbelievers. The Catholic patient has a right to enjoy the benefits of this sacrament which is an enormously valuable gift, of the Lord and of the Church, to sufferers. Medical staff should offer this gift to patients, not only when they are close to death, but also, if the latter wish it, before a major operation, and when they are fighting serious illnesses like tumours, in need of, or in recovery from transplants, and when they are in the Intensive Care Unit. At such times should the chaplain be called upon 'to comfort those being tested by sickness'.[29] The priest prepares the patient with a brief catechesis, administers the sacrament in the name of the Church, and prays in the name of the Lord Jesus Christ the healer.

There is a great deal more to discuss on this subject, for example, the pastoral care of sick children, catechesis of the patient, or the hospital carers, the pastoral council, volunteers, funerals, ecumenism etc., but I shall limit myself to what has been expounded in this present chapter.

I shall conclude with a reflection by Monsignor Antonio Riboldi, a courageous bishop who spoke out against the Mafia, written, while he was still bishop of Acerra near Naples, for the house organ of the San Raffaele 'Sanare Infirmos', which I have edited for many years: 'Permeating the corridors, offices, treatment and analysis areas is an aura which suggests that the San Raffaele is more than just a hospital for treating people's physical ailments, but it is also a centre of education to Life: it embodies what Christ meant when he said, "I am the Life". Through proper religious care, the stupendous chapels which speak only of life, the efforts of the medical staff who work night and day, and the patients themselves, the hospital is made a "Cathedral of pain and love" where the most beautiful celebration of the Eucharist takes place. It is a Eucharistic celebration which does none other than impart serenity and life to those who place themselves in the care of this hospital, just as the moribund traveller in the parable of the Good Samaritan entrusted himself to the care of the Samaritan.'

NOTES

1   Mt 10:6-8.
2   Mt 25:31-34.
3   Lk 13:7.
4   Lk 19:38.
5   Gen 1:26.
6   Mt 25:40.
7   Benedict XVI, *Deus Caritas est*, 33.
8   Lk 5:12.
9   2 Cor 5:14.
10 Cf. Gal 5, 6.
11 Benedict XVI, *Deus Caritas est*, 33.
12 Medical-Prieshood Movement, Milan, 2004, p. 42.
13 Benedict XVI, *Deus Caritas est*, 22.
14 Lk 7:50.
15 Jn 8:11.
16 S. Leone, *The Theological Perspective in Bioethics*, p. 486.
17 Benedict XVI, *Deus Caritas est*, 13.
18 E. Bianchi, L. Manicardi, *Living With the Sick*, Qiqajon, Magnano (BI), 2000, p. 65.
19 Job 19:13-19.
20 Mk 1:40-45.
21 Apostolic exhortation *Familiaris consortio*, 77, Vatican Library, Vatican City 1981.
22 Ibid., 79, 84.
23 *Catechism of the Catholic Church*, 478.
24 Lk 9:23.
25 Apostolic Letter *Salvifici doloris*, 26, Vatican Library, Vatican City, 1984.
26 *Catechism of the Catholic Church*, 1303.
27 Jas 5:14-15.
28 B. McKenna and H. Libersat, *Miracles Do Happen*, Veritas Publications, Dublin, 1987.
29 *Catechism of the Catholic Church*, 1511.

CHAPTER 8

THE CHRISTIAN MEANING OF SUFFERING

Who can forget the last months of the life of Pope John Paul II? In St Peter's Square and on our TV screens he appeared as an exemplar of suffering. He suffered *like* all men and *for* all men, and the sick saw him as one of their own. The Pope, who had written a beautiful apostolic letter on suffering, *Salvifici doloris*, suffered increasingly each day. Medicine proved ineffective and the Lord wanted him in Paradise.

I had never before seen a man of such great stature through whom I could see the face of Christ since he was the Vicar of Christ. I was greatly struck by the televised image of Karol Wojtyla praying, alone, in the private chapel at the Colosseum during the Way of the Cross, written and conducted by Cardinal Joseph Ratzinger, who would later succeed him as Pope Benedict XVI.

John Paul II, like Christ, was walking up his own Mount Calvary, and like Christ he was carrying his cross of suffering. He lived in Christ's love and died after a long period of suffering to be one day resurrected with Christ.

The main thoughts of the Way of the Cross recited by Cardinal Ratzinger were, in fact, words pronounced by Christ in reply to a question made by some Greeks who wished to get to know him, immediately after his entry into Jerusalem: 'Unless a wheat grain falls on the ground and dies, it remains only a single grain; but if it dies, it yields a rich harvest.'[1] We may view the life of John Paul II from this perspective: even beyond the significance of his glorious pontificate, his suffering and death have borne 'a rich harvest'. People are already talking of 'miracles', and the word that John Paul was a saint, heard on the piazza at the time of his death, still echoes strongly around the world. God's people await his canonisation.

ST BENEDICT'S CROSS

A famous actress felt terrified at the thought of having a malign tumour and entered a church just before her appointment with her doctor. Here she read the following words for the first time: 'Your Eternal Father who looks after you today, will look after you tomorrow and every day. He will save you from suffering or give you the strength to overcome it. Therefore find your peace once more and put aside all thoughts of anxiety.' These words of St Francis de Sales seemed to have been written with her in mind, and stayed in her memory.

From that moment on, the woman abandoned herself to God, trusting him to help her face her eventual suffering. She had not been given good news by her doctor, and she suffered a great deal, but the pain served only to strengthen and increase her faith: she trusted God as a child trusts her father, and lost her fear of pain. She always wore St Benedict's cross, which gave her the courage, enlightenment and the faith to accept her suffering gladly. Such Christian bearing and fortitude are rarely witnessed, although in my long years of experience with the sick I have observed that this cross always gives comfort to those faced with evil.

SUFFERING IS NOT A PUNISHMENT

It is necessary at this point to address some mistaken ideas on suffering. One such idea is that God sends suffering to punish us. The Church teaches that we should resign ourselves to God's will and accept suffering. We should not, however, view it as a divine punishment. In the early days of the outbreak of AIDS, one cardinal declared that this illness was a 'plague', a 'scourge' and a 'punishment from God'. Many of us spoke out against this assertion and retorted that a man of the Church should never condemn others, especially in the knowledge that Christ was always compassionate towards those who were ill.

Christ himself corrected his disciples when they asked: 'Rabbi, who sinned, this man or his parents, for him to have been born blind?' Jesus immediately replied: 'Neither he nor his parents sinned;

he was born blind so that the works of God might be displayed in him.'[2] God does not punish or inflict illness on people in the forms of blindness, tumours, AIDS, earthquakes or tsunamis. The opposite is true. God's glory and love are manifested in the avoidance of such evils and the cure of such illnesses.

I find beauty in the words of the neurologist Oliver Sacks in the film *Awakenings* (1990) when he says: 'Naturally, the last thing anybody would do is to provoke illness for the sake of experiencing it. But when illness and accidents do happen, they cause us to think the most profound thoughts and reach the most logical conclusion possible.'

The relatives of patients often ask me: 'Why is there so much suffering?' or 'Why does God permit good people to suffer so much pain?' Such questions pose a paradox. Often, pain and suffering raise doubts about the existence or the presence of God, though in many cases they bring us closer to him and people who are ill come to terms with the idea that their condition is the will of God. Usually, doubts about God are expressed as an outpouring of pent-up emotions and should not be taken at face value. It is in fact certain that such expressions of doubt are a manifestation of real emotional suffering. There are no words to comfort a child who has lost his mother or a husband who has lost his wife.

Death and suffering must be met with humane compassion, and life must go on in faith and hope and on the strength of the good memories which remain with the living. I have observed that at times the best way to cope with emotion, listen to the will of God and turn tears and pain into positive action is through silence.

During times of mourning and suffering it is best to meet doubts on God's existence with silence. There is, truly, very little to be said, but a great deal of meditation to be done. In a godless world, doubt comes easily, but we must not forget that God is always present with us, and more so in our moments of suffering. Moreover, it is pain and suffering which test our way of life: if relationships with others are not quite happy this is the moment to find tranquillity of body and soul.

Over the many years I have spent working in a hospital, I have tried to reach a logical explanation for the mystery of pain. Pain is certainly not a good thing, and it is wrong to urge anybody to accept it passively, for the patient must fight pain with all his might and with an animation borne of faith in God. Pain and suffering are a part of life's mystery.

WHY MUST I SUFFER?

At times, people who have faced or witnessed suffering harden their hearts. I know an elderly person who always blamed God for starvation in some parts of the world when he saw it on TV, or for natural disasters like earthquakes. This is a mistaken attitude, and faith has taught this person to search his own conscience rather than pointing fingers at God.

In the *Confessions* St Augustine too asked, 'Where does evil lie?' and what are 'the roots and seeds of evil'?[3] He found his answer in God's omnipotence and perfect goodness; but evil is ever a mystery to mankind. The problem of why evil exists has always exercised the understanding of the Church, but so far it is still a mystery. As John Paul II states in his apostolic letter *Salvifici doloris*, even mankind 'is an insoluble mystery in his suffering'.[4]

As we saw through the suffering of John Paul II himself, the words of his apostolic letter state that the area of human suffering is much vaster (than medical science suggests), much more varied and multidimensional. Mankind suffers in various ways, not all of which are provided for by medical science, even in its most advanced specialisations. Suffering is 'a great deal broader' than illness, 'more complex and more deeply rooted in our very humanity'.[5]

'Sacred Scripture is a *book about suffering*,' according to the Pope, and he cites many examples and events from it 'which bear witness to suffering, most of all, suffering of an emotional nature'. He lists 'the fear of death' that Ezekiel[6] felt; 'the death of one's offspring' which Agar[7] feared, and 'most of all the death of one's first-born and only child', as Anna, the mother of Tobias,[8] was anxious about; and then 'loneliness and being abandoned by all' as happened to Job.

All the above-listed examples of suffering and many others are still to be met in today's world, especially in hospitals. Pain and suffering take over the whole of the person, because physical suffering which 'pains the body' comes together with psychological suffering – the 'pain of the soul'.[9] Our physical health depends on our having a healthy mind and spirit: the Latin aphorism *'mens sana in corpore sano'* is perfectly true. We need also remember that we are not the true owners of our own bodies; they belong to God who has entrusted them to our care in order that they may be 'temples' for our spirits. Physical health is at the forefront of modern preoccupations: everybody is very health conscious and doing everything possible to stay healthy. There is absolutely nothing wrong with this, but we should not become slaves to it, and above all we must not be too taken in by all the publicity surrounding the industry which purports to care so much for our physical well-being, for it is easy to lose one's soul in the attempt to save one's body.

WHAT IS EVIL?

In *Salvifici doloris* the Pope attempts to answer the question on the essence of evil in a concise manner. The third section of the apostolic letter bears the title: 'In search of an answer to the question on the meaning of suffering'. As with the question on the essence of evil, the Pope also attempts to answer the question on the meaning and the reason for human suffering. 'This question is most heartfelt in the Book of Job.'[10] I agree perfectly with Job when he remonstrates against his friend's statements that suffering is 'a just evil' because it is a 'punishment for transgression, sin and crime'. Job could not accept this as an explanation for his suffering because 'he knows that he has done nothing to deserve such punishment, and to show this he talks about all the good things he has accomplished in his lifetime. In the end God himself scolds Job's friends for their accusations and acknowledges that Job is not guilty of anything. He is an innocent victim whose suffering must be accepted as a mystery which cannot be rationalised'.[11]

This is the moral principle which should guide all pastoral workers in the field of healthcare. At times one would like to comfort the sick by saying that everything (illness included) happens by the will of God, but this is rather a paternalistic or patronising attitude which does nothing to reconcile a patient who is in a state of shock, anger and denial at learning of his illness.[12] When we approach a patient who is still under the initial shock of learning of his illness, it is advisable to avoid encouraging him to resign himself to the will of God, even when we do talk of suffering.

Jesus never told those who were ill to resign themselves to their illness; as a monk from the Bosé monastery, Fr Luciano Manicardi, writes, 'Christ never says that suffering brings us closer to God, he never asks the sick to offer up their suffering to God, but always fights against evil, and prays for the curing of illness'.[13]

The Prior of Bosé monastery, Fr Enzo Bianchi, reminds us that 'the Christian sense' of suffering occurs in the meeting between the Holy Spirit, and the personality of the person who is ill, his faith and his environment. This is why, when we write or speak of illness and of the spiritual attitude with which to confront it, we need to avoid dogmatic categorical statements and making statements beginning with 'one must' or 'this must be' etc. This is not merely a matter of using the correct language, but a matter of respecting the free will of the person involved, in what must be an event resulting from the enlightenment of that person by the Holy Spirit and sustained by the faith, within the limits and conditions imposed by his illness.[14]

THE CONVERSION OF CLARA BOOTHE LUCE

In the initial phase of counselling, when faced with the question, 'Why has God struck me with this illness?' I always answer truthfully, 'I'm sorry, but I don't know', or, 'I've come across many things in life which can't be explained'. Sometimes I have also added: 'Let's see if we can find the answer to that together.' This is not an evasion of the question itself; it is simply a way of avoiding giving a glib reply on a subject as mysterious as suffering. Added to that, it also shows the patient that there are no ready-made answers to this profound question.

The first American woman ambassador to Italy, in the early 1950s, was Clara Boothe Luce, the wife of Henry Luce, founder-editor of *Time* magazine. The Italian people and press of the time were very interested in her because she was the first woman to occupy such an important office after the war, and also because she was a fervent Catholic, a writer, and a very amiable person. However, few probably knew the path that had led her to faith.

Mrs Boothe Luce had had an only daughter who had been given a sports car by her parents on her eighteenth birthday. The girl had been thrilled with her present and drove around rather too fast in it, as young people will. Sadly, she was involved in a fatal traffic accident shortly after. This naturally threw her mother into a dark depression and she was constantly questioning the reason for her daughter's death. One day she asked Bishop Fulton Sheen (whose beatification is now in process) about it. At that time he was a household name, known to all through his TV programme, *Life is Worth Living*. His answer to Clara was, 'I don't know why such things happen. You must find the answer within yourself'. This was the beginning of the spiritual journey which led Clara to the faith.

CHRIS CAPPELL'S MUSICAL GENIUS

Another experience which has left an impression on me is that which involved the parents of Chris Cappell. Born Christian Cappelluti, in Rome in 1975, only son of Franco and Adriana Cappelluti, Christian grew up in the EUR district of Rome[15] and attended the Jesuit Collegio Massimo, after which he went to Wake Forest University in North Carolina from where he graduated with honours in Economics. Subsequently he studied musical composition at Berklee College of Music in Boston, where the sons and daughters of many famous singers studied.

At the age of eight he had received a guitar (which he christened Katy) as a Christmas present from his parents, and he had learnt to play it by ear, following the method of David L. Burge. At age twenty, Christian collaborated with the well-known Italian singer Mina on an album entitled *Pappa di Latte* (1995); two years previously he had joined the Pooh[16] on tour. One member of the band, Red Canzian, would later say: 'Chris was an absolute genius and he was different from other people in the profundity of his thought and feeling – I once thought of him as a kind of John Lennon.'

Fr Antonio Spadaro SJ, editor of the bi-weekly journal *Catholic Civilization*, who had known Chris during his school days at 'the Massimo', and who organised the compilation of his songs, wrote this about him in the introduction to his book *Let Me Run Away*: Christian's most prominent qualities were his creativity, his imagination and his ability to feel inspiration.' Mina said of him: 'When he was in the USA Chris had a great career ahead of him. He was one of those uncommon young people who give one hope for a better future for this world. I loved him dearly and admired his passion for music, which I share.'

But tragically, Chris died suddenly during a holiday in Scotland, struck down by a food allergy on 9 August 1998. His parents barely managed to reach Scotland before his death. The loss of their only son was a great blow to them, but they found the strength to react positively: they had a college built in Anzio, where Chris used to spend his holidays, and where he is buried beneath a cross encircled with a wreath, in the American fashion. The Chris Cappell College specialising in classical studies, presented to the community of Anzio by Adriana and Franco Cappelluti, is the most beautiful building of its kind in Italy and can hold 750 students. This generous act has enabled Chris' parents to keep their son's memory alive.

Chris still lives on through his parents' love; through his beautiful songs (some titles which come to mind are: 'Poor boy', 'Constance', 'Lemon Girl', 'Close your eyes' and 'Let me run away'; there are many others), and in the hearts of those young people attending the college, whose presence honours his memory daily.[17]

Chris himself wrote, 'It is only through faith in God and in ourselves that we can fill up the void, the dark places in our minds'.[18] His parents have told me that Chris valued righteousness and attempted to live by ethical rules. It may therefore be observed in both Clare Boothe Luce's case and in that of Chris Cappell's parents that 'the harvest of illness and tragedy is often goodness' as stated in the Book of Proverbs. 'For Yahweh reproves the man he loves, as a father checks a well-loved son.'[19]

As has been explained earlier, God does not punish, or impose evil and torments on mankind, for God is love; as Benedict XVI states in his encyclical: 'God's love for us is a fundamental question in our lives and a decisive factor in the discovery of who God is and who we are.'[20]

We should not lay the blame for illnesses like cancer or AIDS, blindness or even violent events like terrorism and war, at God's door. Patients will often say, 'I've lived a good life and do not deserve this illness God has sent me'. But the sick person does not suffer alone; Christ suffers with him, in him and for him. We read this in the fourth part of the apostolic letter *Salvifici doloris*, where John Paul II wrote that Christ overcame suffering with love: 'God so loved the world that he gave his only Son so that whoever believes in him will not die, but will have eternal life.'[21] With these words of Jesus to Nicodemus does the Pope introduce the *salvific act of God*.

As we are reminded by the crucifix, which some people want to have banished from hospitals, court rooms and schools, Christ was surrounded by suffering during his three years of public life: 'He walked about doing good works.'[22] Christ was sensitive to any form of illness and on three separate occasions restored the dead to life; he also wept for his dead friend Lazarus. Christ lived among people and their suffering: 'He cured the sick, consoled the grief-stricken, fed the hungry, freed men from deafness and blindness, from leprosy and demonic possession and from various physical disabilities.'[23] Indeed, he spent more time in healing than he did in preaching.

Often, while I'm walking through the hospital corridors, I think of Jesus and pray that he 'might pass this way, doing good works' with my sick people. When I was given the grace to see the Blessed Mother Teresa among the crowds of lepers in Calcutta, I felt the presence of Christ among them very strongly. The same feeling came to me on many other occasions: at San Giovanni Rotondo when St Pio da Pietralcina was blessing the sick; when the Blessed George Preca, founder of the Society for Christian Doctrine in Malta, was among the sick;[24] with the Blessed Pope John XXIII and Pope John Paul II among the children in the Christ Child Hospital in Rome; at the bedside of Monsignor Luigi Guissani, founder of Communion and Freedom, when he was a patient at the San Raffaele; with Don Luigi Di Liegro, founder of the Rome branch of Caritas; with Monsignor Pietro Fiordelli, bishop of Prato, who was afflicted with a malign tumour; and among the patients of the San Raffaele hospital. This is not merely my imagination at work. I believe it is a true phenomenon and I pray that I may be given the grace of bringing Christ among the sick.

The important truth is that Christ was not only physically close to the sick, but 'he took their suffering upon himself'.[25] He experienced all kinds of suffering, those stemming from poverty and misery; marginalisation; the incomprehension of others, apart from his suffering on the cross. But on the third day he rose again.

THE SONG OF THE SERVANT OF JHWH

Among the various messianic texts of the Old Testament which 'foretold the sufferings of the future Anointed Son of God' the Pope presents us with the 'fourth poem of the Servant of JHWH', found in the Book of Isaiah, the 'fifth evangelist'.[26]

'This,' writes John Paul II, 'is how the true man of sorrows is presented to us: he is not handsome or attractive to us in a visual sense … He is scorned and rejected by men, *the sorrowful man* who is well familiar with the endurance of suffering, like one we would hide our faces from, he was scorned and we had no regard for him. Despite this, he took our sufferings upon himself *and put on our sorrows*, and we judged him wanting and worthy of punishment, beaten and humiliated by God. His side was pierced with a spear for our crimes, he was crushed for our iniquity. The punishment which saves us was visited upon him; we have been healed on account of his wounds. Each one of us was as a lost sheep, each followed his own solitary path; *the Lord visited our iniquity upon him.*'[27]

It was the thought of these lines which moved John Paul II so deeply, and why he was so greatly impressed by Mel Gibson's film *The Passion of the Christ.* The realism captured in this film touched millions of Christians and non-Christians throughout the world, and has even brought about the conversion of people who were moved by the terrible suffering of Christ, who gave unto the last drop of his blood for us on the Cross.[28] Those who thought the film too 'horrific' and 'bloody' are unfamiliar with the song of Isaiah.

The Man on the Cross is the Only Son of the Father: 'God from God.' He is the Lamb of God who has taken away all the sins of the world by taking them upon himself and this is 'the true cause of the Redeemer's suffering'. He suffers 'voluntarily and innocently'.[29] His prayer was: 'My Father, if it is possible, let this cup pass me by. Nevertheless, let it be as you, not I, would have it.'[30]

PRAYING FOR HEALING

With a contrite spirit and in the light of faith, that God may heal them in body, mind and spirit, the sick have a right to pray for healing. One may bring to mind the echoing chorus of millions of faithful pilgrims to Lourdes: 'Lord, give me sight', 'Lord, let me walk' and 'Lord, if it be your will, I may be healed'. The sick may, like Job, pray to God to free them from evil. The sick are the embodiment of the suffering Christ. 'Seeing the faith'[31] of those who pray on their sickbeds, Christ may allow their healing; the sick ask for 'the cup' of suffering to be taken away from them.

The sick go on pilgrimage to Lourdes, Fatima, Medjugorie and other Marian sanctuaries around the world in order to ask for healing, if not of the body, that of the soul. There are many attestations of healings having taken place at these sanctuaries where, '*together with Mary*, Mother of Christ, who stood *beneath the Cross*, we stand, by all the crosses of contemporary mankind'.[32]

NOTES

1   Jn 12:24.
2   Jn 9:3.
3   St Augustine *Confessions*, VI, 1, 5.
4   *Salvifici doloris*, 5.
5   *Salvifici doloris*, 5.
6   Isa 38:1-3.
7   Gen 15-16.
8   Tob 10:1-17.
9   *Salvifici doloris*, 5.
10   Ibid., 10.
11   Ibid., 11.
12   E. Kübler Ross, *Death and Dying*.
13   E. Bianchi and L. Manicardi, *Living with the Sick*, pp. 77–8.
14   Ibid. pp. 15–16.
15   The EUR district takes its name from the acronym for 'Esposizione Universale di Roma'. It is also known as the Europa district, and is the 32nd district of Rome, to be found in the south of the city. The district was originally designed to house the Universal Exposition of 1942 celebrating the twentieth anniversary of the Fascist March on Rome, symbolising the rise to power of the Fascists. However the exhibition was cancelled because of the Second World War, and the district, still under construction when the war broke out, was completed in later years.
16   A popular and highly respected Italian band.
17   I strongly recommend reading the book *Let Me Run Away*, by Antonio Spadaro SJ, Edizioni Messaggero, Padova, 2001. It contains the lyrics of Chris Cappell's songs both in English and Italian. Anybody interested in obtaining the original songs may email: info@chriscappell.com.
18   E. Guerriero, ed., *Testimonies of the Italian Catholic Church. Nineteenth Century to the Present*, San Paolo; Cinisello Balsamo, Milan (2006), p. 405.
19   Prov 3:12.
20   Benedict XVI, *Deus Caritas est*, 2.
21   John Paul II, *Apostolic Letter Salvifici doloris*, 14.
22   Acts 10:38.
23   *Salvifici doloris*, 16.
24   A. Montonati *Courage and Prophecy. Blessed George Preca (Malta 1880-1962) – a Pioneer of Vatican II*, San Paolo, Cinisello Balsamo, Milan, 2003.
25   *Salvifici doloris*, 16.
26   Isa 53:2-6.
27   *Salvifici doloris*, 17.
28   Monsignor Carmel Psaila, Maltese national poet in his 'T'adoriam Ostia Divina' ,'We Adore You, Divine Host', written for the occasion of the International Eucharistic Congress held in Malta in 1913.
29   *Salvifici doloris*, 18.
30   Mt 26:39.
31   Mt 9:2.
32   *Salvifici doloris*, 31.

CHAPTER 9

AT THE BEDSIDE OF THE DYING

About thirty years ago, while I was working in Milan with the widely circulated weekly magazine *The Christian Family* I received a phone call late one night. A woman with a markedly foreign accent told me, between sobs, the story of her fifty-year-old marriage. Her husband had been a professional and she had been ill with a tumour. They had travelled to the United States and France for her treatment, which entailed enormous expense. Now they were penniless and survived on bread and coffee. They had neither children nor relatives. I did not immediately understand what it was the woman wanted of me and I offered to go and visit and give whatever help she needed. However, she was too embarrassed to give me their home address or telephone number. During subsequent phone calls I insisted on being given their address, even offering to send money by post. She would have none of it: her answer was always, 'Thank you, but no'. In all this time the couple had confined themselves to their home.

About a week later, returning to Milan from Prato by train, I read in the paper: 'Elderly Couple Found Lying in Each Other's Arms in Attempted Suicide.'

I was startled by this news and felt guilty at the thought that I could have acted to avert this tragedy. Since they had both been hospitalised at the Polyclinic, I went to visit them: first him, in the male wing, and then her. They were both tearful; they had wanted to die because, they kept saying, 'there is nothing left for us to live for'. I took care of them to the end of their lives: one of the greatest difficulties was finding an old people's home where they could be together to the end. But there was no room anywhere except against payment.

What saddened me most of all was their total lack of desire to live, and their decision to 'die together' at any cost. As there was nobody to look after them, the only thing to be done was for me to care for them in accordance with Christ's command in the parable of the Good Samaritan: 'Go, and do the same yourself'.[1]

Their death by suicide would have been a horrible tragedy, but only God knows what they had been going through. I was mostly struck not by their tragic gesture, but by the love and closeness which they had shared throughout their years of marriage. It was not my place to judge them, but I was certain when they died, a few months apart, that God, who loves us both as a Mother and a Father, received them with open arms.

They had freely chosen death, if it is possible to choose freely when one's mind and body are embroiled in the turmoil of such violent emotions as theirs had been. They had wanted to renounce the gift of life because this had become meaningless to them who had once wanted for nothing: it now seemed like an endless succession of days spent in poverty. They felt totally bereft, without the light of anybody's smile, or the warmth of kindness, and crushed by shame; but they had complete faith in God's understanding and forgiveness of their desperate action.

DEATH: THE LAST TABOO

Nowadays death is one of the few remaining taboos in the western world. It is viewed by doctors as the failure of their art and that of the patient in their struggle against pain and illness. When a patient dies, especially so in the case of one who has had a long relationship with his doctor, the latter questions his own death. Faced with death he feels impotent. Some doctors, in particular those treating patients with AIDS or cancer, have vented their feelings to me, confessing that they had done their utmost to save their patients even knowing that death is unavoidable.

The link between death and medicine is so complex that, despite our faith, it throws us into crisis. To the end one must fight to preserve life without, however, resorting to extraordinary treatments or, on the other hand, euthanasia. The latter has been defined as 'the illusion of a kind death' by Milan Archbishop Dionigi Tettamanzi, which the 'culture of death' is trying to exalt and legalise, considering it a human right to decide how and when one should end one's existence.

Both extremes, on the one hand the preservation of life by extraordinary means, and on the other euthanasia, are anti-ethical. Euthanasia has always been a problem, but it is only since the mid-1950s that new and intensive medical interventions have been used to make both euthanasia and the preservation of life at all costs the final struggle against death.

The person who is close to death, whether or not in his full mental capacity, should be considered a person to the very end. This is one of the reasons why the Church does not accept active euthanasia under any circumstances. It also condemns a persistence in the preservation of life at all costs, which involves extraordinary medical interventions.

However, in this context, rather than ethical questions related to euthanasia we are interested in the ethical care of the dying – 'being close to' and 'looking after' the patient, not only from the perspective of medical personnel and the clergy, but also that of members of the patient's family.

In his book *Caring for the Sick to the End*,[2] Massimo Petrini writes: 'In the fifteenth century, at the height of humanism, a new literary genre gained in popularity and spread rapidly, probably starting in southern Germany, this was the *Ars Moriendi* (The Art of Dying).' 'It is as yet unknown', says the author, 'who began this movement, but there is good evidence to place its roots in eastern Germany during the time of the Council of Costanza (1414–1418), and furthermore, within the Dominican order.'[3]

When I was a child, and even an adolescent in Malta, I remember the practice of taking collections 'for a holy death' against the promise of masses celebrated for the soul of the donor. The money thus collected was then used for the upkeep of some orphanage or other. This was also a common practice in Italy, especially in central and southern regions, where active fraternities dedicated themselves to collecting alms for such worthy causes.

St Francis of Assisi called death 'sister' despite the fact that sudden death, as opposed to 'a holy death' in one's own bed and surrounded by one's family, had for centuries been considered almost a punishment from God. St Joseph is invoked as the protector of the 'holy death'. In the litany of the saints, which was once recited much more frequently than it is today, people sang: 'From sudden death protect us, Lord.' The Sacrament of the Sick used to be called 'Extreme Unction' and was often administered with scepticism (as also happens today) or simply to satisfy popular belief, to people who were at the point of death. The sung funeral masses; processions accompanying the priest carrying the Viaticum; Gregorian masses (those celebrated for thirty consecutive days for the repose of the souls of the dead); floral wreaths and invitations to mourners to donate money for 'good causes'; marble or bronze monuments in cemeteries; the wearing of black; the slow tolling of bells signalling the impending death of a parishioner; horse-drawn hearses; and many other rites are not only cultural traditions, but signs of the respect accorded the dead.

How do people die in hospitals?

With time, customs and rites have changed, but respect for the dead is still manifest, whether people are believers or not, and whether or not they are practising Catholics. During my funeral homilies I always make a point of thanking the relatives and friends, both Catholic and non-Catholic, and attempt to add a few comforting words, as I did during the funeral of an intellectual who had been a non-believer. One day somebody thanked me for this, saying, 'You have touched my heart'. Another person told me that he had parted company with the Church when still a young man, after his father had been refused a Christian burial by the parish priest because he had committed suicide. I had been aware of similar reactions by people in Malta, when the Church refused burial in consecrated ground close to the Addolorata cemetery to a man who had been a leader of the Socialist Party, which was at odds with the Church. These are still painful hurts for which the Church has asked pardon.

In recent years much has changed. Vatican Council II[4] and, more recently, the *Catechism of the Catholic Church* have endowed Christian death with a Christ-centred significance. To the Christian, death is the desire to be free of the body in order to be with Christ[5] who has overcome death and returned to a new life.[6] Therefore all believers in Christ are destined for immortality through resurrection 'since death came into existence through a man, so also will the resurrection of the dead'.[7]

The prayer of the fourteenth-century St Gregory of Nyssa has always inspired me for this reason: 'you have turned our fear of death to hope; you have changed the end of our life into a beginning of our true life. You let our bodies rest for a while and reawaken them. You entrust our bodies to the earth to resurrect them to eternal beauty. To those who are afraid you have given the sign of the cross, which is an assurance of life.'

The changes referred to earlier began to come about partly because of the fact that more people were dying in hospitals and old people's homes. People often die alone in hospital, without any privacy, and quite often without the comfort of a priest nearby. Relatives often receive a phone call in which they are bluntly told to come to the hospital as their 'father is dying' or even informed that the patient has died.

I am very unhappy about the way people are sometimes left to die in hospital and the lack of love or respect which is shown to the families of the deceased. Once upon a time, in hospitals run by religious, as in Malta – the 'Blue Sisters' hospital was run by a society of English and Irish nursing sisters – two nuns would always be praying at the bedside of a dying patient. I was also favourably impressed by the care given to dying patients in the Lutheran hospital of Chicago.

When Cardinal Carlo Maria Martini was archbishop of Milan, he frequently denounced the way people were left to 'die alone in hospitals' in an anonymous and cold atmosphere. This is an ethical problem – people must be shown respect until they breathe their last. At the 'Milano Medicina' conference, Cardinal Martini had this to say: 'Ethics and solidarity have foundered because of the charging of medical fees and consequent abuses, uncivilized hospital care, bureaucratisation, and the shirking of responsibility by the health service.'

On the pretext of respecting the patients' privacy (carried to the extreme of denying a priest information about which ward one of his own parishioners is in!) the dying person is left to face death all alone. There is no time for feelings in hospital; often the patient sharing a room with a dying person is forced to witness his roommate's final moments and suffer in empathy. The staff are unprepared to comfort dying patients, or do not have the time to, and at times may be unable to master their own emotions. Doctors come and go, feeling unable to help, and many will visit without uttering a word. The hospital chaplain, who may already have administered the Sacrament of the Sick, cannot spend all his time with the one patient; unless the latter is somebody close to him he will not sit up with him all night. Even funerals take place in the little chapel adjoining the cold, gloomy mortuary, with little ceremony, and far-removed from the familiarity of the deceased's parish.

One of the reasons for these changes for the worse is the secularisation of a society, which in some northern European countries is termed 'post-Christian'. The ethicist Robert M. Veatch claims that this is the result of a 'biological revolution' which has influenced philosophical, ethical, legal and socio-political thinking.[8] This revolution has been advanced by intensive therapy techniques which, it must be said, have greatly benefited mankind and science: nowadays, seven out of ten patients admitted into the emergency department survive, despite much suffering, thanks to techniques like tube-feeding and mechanical blood-circulation or breathing aids. In such cases ethics demands that we do not underestimate the suffering of the patient, who feels out of touch with normality.

How the patient feels
Nobody can describe better than a patient how one feels in such a situation. In his book *A Return to Life*, Emilio Bonicelli, who was diagnosed with leukaemia quite by chance and battled the disease,

describes his experiences: 'After my transplant I was kept in a sterilised room into which my wife and children could only come wearing protective caps, gowns, booties and masks. For a whole month I could only see the eyes above the masks of those who tended me: looks of love and empathy which encouraged me to overcome my illness and be reborn. Hospital patients normally have a TV to help them pass the time. I did not. I had brought a picture. It is the reproduction of an old painting of the Madonna and child Jesus: a fifteenth-century fresco in which Christ, still in swaddling, is stretching out his little hand to caress his mother's face. "A picture instead of a TV?" I was asked. Everybody thought me mad. However, it was a challenge I'd laid upon myself: how many hours could I bear to spend in this austere room listening to the incessant hum of the air conditioner? Will I be bored to death without a TV? Perhaps. However, I do have a CD player for listening to music and a radio for news. I hold firm to my determination not to have a TV. In the end I will find that I had been right to do so.'[9]

ACCOMPANYING THE DYING

Faced with such situations one asks oneself what one can do on both human and ethical levels. This is not an easy question: I found the best answer from Cecily Saunders, the originator of the hospice. Hospices are institutions in which people suffering from cancer may live out their last months or weeks. Saunders would say to cancer patients: 'We care about you because of who you are and you are worth caring for to the last moments of your lives. We will do all we can not only to make your death more comfortable, but also to help you live a full life to the very end.'

How did Cecily Saunders and her staff keep this promise? They 'accompanied' the sick, supporting them every step of the way day after day, and providing them with loving care and empathy: this is the true meaning of the ethical care of hospital patients on a daily basis. Ethical care is a way of accompanying patients along the road to death.

It was the French and Belgian bishops who first used the term 'accompaniment', which has a meaning that goes beyond mere attendance. They stressed that 'a proper idea of the accompaniment of the dying presupposes the rediscovery of the profound significance of death. We tend to think of things technically, assuming we always have the upper hand and can solve all problems. However, faced with death we cannot do this, because death is a mystery that may only be approached in silence and with humility. Death cannot be "solved" by means of scientific competence: for it takes us into the sphere of the sacred and of the mysterious presence of God. It is the final experience of living, the one which constrains us to leave everything behind and forget our compulsive need to dominate everything. Why do we consider euthanasia so much nowadays? Perhaps because, even on a purely philosophical level, we have lost the authentically human sense of death. We give in to the temptation of considering death a scientific problem which we must solve.'[10]

Death is a 'mystery' which cannot be confronted with medical science alone. The accompaniment of the dying person is a sacred act of love and humanity which brings us closer to Christ, who mourned the death of his friend Lazarus. Doctors and nurses tend to the patient but it is often the priest, the family and volunteers who accompany him or her. When there is no longer anything to be done from a medical perspective, and all hope of recovery is lost, accompaniment is the final form of care for the sick person. 'When there is no longer anything to be done, there is plenty to do,' as went the slogan of the Italian Cancer Society.

ELIMINATING THE USE OF THE WORD 'TERMINAL'

The phrase 'a terminally ill patient' used by the mass media, in the medical sphere, and even in the Charter of Health Workers,[11] is a misnomer.

I remember the words of writer Gaspare Barbiellini Amidei during a round table conference organised by 'Medicine and Human Science' of the San Raffaele (Milan) hospital: 'I believe that it has always been clear, at least theoretically, to every doctor, to every person, that certainly there are people who are incurable, but I really wish that the phrase "terminally ill", which smacks rather too much of something mechanical, like train stations or disused railway tracks, were no longer used by the medical profession and in debate. If this phrase, which is so suggestive of a train carriage travelling down a dead-end track, were no longer to be used of a patient who might be incurable, yes, but not beyond care, it would be no bad thing. At times, as the philosophers say, words can be as painful as stones.'

Massimo Pietrini also writes on this subject: 'The English phrase "terminally ill" literally translated into Italian as "malato terminale" does not have an equivalent meaning, but only bears some similarity of sound; as with "dying" and "moribund" which mean respectively "he who is about to die and therefore has biological, clinical and medical symptoms which will lead to a rapid death without immediate medical intervention" and "he who is destined to die soon, despite any therapeutic treatment which may be given".'[12]

These comments remind us that the dying are persons created 'in the image and likeness of God'. To the very end of life, and even after, when all that remains is the body, these people must be accorded their proper dignity. And it is for the sake of their dignity that they have the right not to mere treatment, but to be ethically accompanied in a humane and spiritual manner so that they can face the crossing into eternal life with serenity and Christian and human dignity. The need to preserve the human dignity of the dying person is often discounted, especially in the case of old people, by both hospital staff and the person's own family.

If hospital staff show any lack of respect for the dying person, the family should report this to the hospital administration or the hospital public relations officer. There is a great deal to learn from the dying: death teaches us a great deal about life itself and it is a privilege for us to witness; it is an opportunity to take stock of our own lives. The 'agony' in the sense of death throes, a word which has fallen out of use nowadays, defines the moment in time when the person begins his or her final journey towards complete union with the Creator.

AGONIA

The final moments of a person's life may bear a rich harvest of wisdom for the person who accompanies the patient, especially so if the dying person is somebody they cherish. Moreover it is a privileged opportunity for showing charity, solidarity and for reflection. The throes of death mark the moment in which the patient is close to the end of life. This involves both physical and psychological suffering, and the spiritual accompaniment of the patient with prayer is an imploration of God's mercy. At such moments I think of 'the agony of Christ'[13] in the Garden of Gethsemane, when he sweated blood and water. This, as the stem of the word derived from the Greek *agon*,[14] meaning struggle, suggests, is a moment of anguish, a struggle of the body and spirit against death, or a duel between life and death.

Who will win? If the hospital is a 'temple', dying there equates with dying in a temple, for God suffers with the dying person. And it is again God who triumphs with the resurrection: if Christ had not risen from death, our faith would be baseless; but he did.[15] Our faith requires us to defend and be witnesses for the value of life up to the last breath, that is, to help unique individual human beings to die at peace.

The accompaniment of a dying person is no easy matter: it brings sorrow, compassion, anguish and a sense of loss, especially if the dying person is someone close. If the accompanying person has faith, he may find comfort in it through prayer and the sacraments. This is a time during which we are compelled to think about our own deaths as an integral part of our lives here and now.

Holistic medicine does not conceive of death as being merely a biological phenomenon, but – with a Christian outlook – it views death as a gateway leading the dying person to meet his Maker. For this reason, the patient has the right to die in dignity and serenity, preferably at home, surrounded by his family, and not alone and uncomforted.

I am in complete agreement with those doctors who advise the family to take a patient home when the person's condition allows it, or when there is nothing more that can be done for that person in hospital. Most patients are very keen to return home and immediately aver to feeling better once they do. Sadly, some people are very much against having sick members of their family dying at home. I remember an elegantly-dressed and bejewelled lady, some years younger than her dying husband, who became incandescent with rage at the suggestion that her husband should return home to die, and insisted, 'I do not want him dying at home'. I later discovered that she had servants at home and cared very much for her dogs.

THE RIGHTS OF THE DYING PERSON

The accompaniment of the sick to the end of their lives should abide by some human and ethical principles, among which are the following:

1. Respect of the dying person according to a personalised ethic and an accompaniment which is unobtrusive. This approach should be taken by all: hospital workers, relatives and volunteers.

2. Never be too invasive of the patient's space: allow time when the room may be left to the patient; this is especially important if the room is shared with one or more patients.

3. Ensure a serene and quiet ambience, that is, avoid too much chatter; turn off the TV; and do not have too many relatives in the room at any time.

4. Hospital staff or family should ask for spiritual assistance i.e. the anointing of the sick, Holy Communion and some moments of prayer.

5. Talk to and pray with the dying person kindly and lovingly, and remind him of God's mercy and the motherly love of Our Lady.

6. Do not be afraid of giving hope to the dying person and of reinforcing his faith, without giving any false hopes.

7. Always respect the patient's mood, culture and religious beliefs.

Many of these proposals, which constitute an active ethic, are carried in the charter for the terminally ill. In this paper are listed the rights of the dying person, among which are many of the principles of person-centred ethics of care: the right to be thought of as an individual up to the very moment of death; the right to information on one's condition if one desires such information; the right to be given honest answers and not be deceived; the right to be given a say in decisions concerning oneself, and the right to have one's desires respected; the right to receive treatment or medication to alleviate pain; the right to continued treatment and care in the location chosen by the dying person; the right not to be made to undergo treatments which merely postpone death, thus prolonging the agony of waiting for death; the right to express one's feelings; the right to psychological care and spiritual comfort according to the dying person's beliefs and religion; the right to have one's loved ones nearby; the right not to have to die in solitude and isolation; the right to a peaceful and dignified death.

The principles proclaimed in the charter concern the ethical attitude of those who accompany the dying, and require that doctors, nurses and seminarists study the *Ars moriendi*, which should be included in medical and nursing studies and pastoral theology. Every university should feel the need to teach this subject in depth; only in this way may the collective taboo on death be overcome. It is only through a study of the *Ars moriendi* that doctors can deepen their knowledge of the human person and of human suffering. As Plato states: 'In order to become a *good doctor* one must first experience suffering.' Professor Giovanni Reale develops this idea with the following observation: 'Plato has therefore perfectly understood that even the great problem of health is resolved when we *learn through pain*, especially the fact that *the body should not only be treated materially but also spiritually*, and this does not only refer to the patient's spirit, but also that of the doctor.'[16]

This Platonic idea must be transmitted convincingly and in a pragmatic manner to medical and nursing students as well as to the many doctors who, despite having taken the Hippocratic oath, lack an ethical conscience and do not respect the value of life in its totality.

TOTAL PAIN

God alone knows the time, the place and the way each of us will die – this is the mystery of life. In the past the faithful were encouraged to pray for a 'good death'. People desired to die without suffering, or, as they used to say, 'in their sleep'. All people are afraid of dying. Even believers are frightened by the thought of that final journey and avoid thinking about it. Even believers have niggling doubts about the hereafter: the fear that this life may be all there is, and after it – a void. Those who have lived without faith, and who have not kept the commandments fear death even more intensely. What we fear most is the unknown rather than the separation from the world and leaving our loved ones behind.

We often refer to death by means of euphemisms in order to camouflage it from ourselves. Our humanity should not be weakened by the wait for death to take place – if we live in the light of the faith, we will be rewarded with resurrection in Christ.

Anthropological studies show that euthanasia is a product of human culture, brought about by our fear of pain and suffering. Added to this is the fear of being abandoned and left to face death alone by a society which hides from the thought of death and pretends to itself that it does not exist.

A positive way of overcoming this mindset which is fertile ground for a pro-euthanasia culture is by creating a 'culture of life' through spiritual, psychological and social accompaniment of the sick. At the moment of 'total suffering', as Cecily Saunders describes it, we need to help the dying person through the 'last lap' of his or her growth by being there for the person, ready to empathise with and listen to him or her and show a great deal of human compassion and love.[17]

According to Elisabeth Kübler Ross, the dying person goes through a number of emotional stages: an initial reaction of shock and negation; non-acceptance; anger; depression; coming to terms; and eventually hope. It is hard for the patient to go from one stage to the next and he needs to be accompanied every step of the way.

There are also patients who bravely face the fact of their impending death. Their bedside is often a place of learning and an altar, as in the case of Rosanna Benzi, who for many years had to live in a steel lung. Such patients are people who believe in the mystery of life and death – this is a great gift from God.

The words of a student nurse afflicted with a serious illness have stayed engraved in my memory. She wrote a letter to her colleagues in which she asked: 'What are you afraid of? It is I who am dying.' The young woman was right to my mind. Many of us are uncomfortable in the presence of somebody who knows he or she is dying, and try to avoid being with that person. What follows is the complete text of the letter:

> I have one to six months of life left, perhaps it might stretch to a year, but nobody wants to talk about it. I find myself faced with a solid wall of silence and solitude – that is all I am left with. I have come to represent that which each of you fears, whatever that is, the fear of that which we all know we must one day face. You slip into my room to give me medication or take my blood pressure, and make your escape no sooner is the duty done. And is it because I too am a student nurse, or is it simply because I'm human, that I am aware of your fear and it feeds my own? What are you afraid of? It is I who am dying. Don't avoid me. Be patient. All I ask is the reassurance of knowing that someone will be here to hold my hand when I need it. I am frightened. Perhaps you are all used to death, but to me it is a new experience. I have never had to die before.[18]

I'd like to refer briefly to the patient's right to be spoken to honestly at this point. Telling a patient the truth about his or her condition is the first step to an authentic and sincere accompaniment. Hiding or disguising the truth, especially when it has been expressly asked for, is no act of love. It is the patient's right to be told the truth and it is the doctor's duty to break the truth gently to the patient. It is unethical to refuse to do this; however one cannot generalise here: it is also important to gauge the patient's ability to deal with the truth and act accordingly.

Kübler Ross systematically interviewed hundreds of gravely ill patients: 'When one really listens to what they have to say, not only can they tell one that they are aware of being close to death, but many of them can also tell when this will happen.'[19] When a patient can express his or her thoughts intelligibly and reasonably clearly, it means that he or she knows what is happening and has not been taken in by the charade being played out at the bedside.[20]

It is, without a doubt, the doctor's duty to tell the patient the truth about his or her condition; this responsibility however should be shared by the nurses, who are closer to the patient and are therefore in a better position to break the news more gradually and humanely. 'The ministrations of the nurse,' states the Code of Ethics of the American Nursing Association, 'are a decisive influence on the way terminal illness is experienced, and on whether or not the patient approaches death peacefully and with dignity.'[21]

THE FINAL DAYS AND HOURS

During the years of violence and bloodshed between Catholics and Protestants in Ireland, some will remember a photograph which had made its way around the world: it was taken in Derry and showed an Irish soldier lying dead on the ground, covered in blood. Crouching beside the soldier's body was a priest who was in the act of wiping away the blood from the dead young man's face with his handkerchief.

Monsignor Edward Daly was bishop of Derry for twenty years. He retired in 1993 for health reasons and is now chaplain of the Foyle Hospice in Derry. In his book *Do Not Let Your Hearts Be Troubled*, which recounts his ten-year experience at the hospice, he writes: 'Having the privilege of spending many hours by the side of a person who has come to the end of his or her earthly journey is a very special grace. When the death of a loved one is imminent the family and friends of the dying person want to be close by. They hover around the bed, at times holding the sick person's hand, talking in hushed and kindly tones, hugging one another. There are long silences punctuated by brief exchanges – for not many words are necessary in such a situation. When the dying person's breathing becomes laboured, they feel an irresistible urge to help their loved one breathe, to breathe with their loved one. It is an extraordinary feeling which only those who have been at the bedside of a dying friend are familiar with. People tiptoe in and out of the room. At times they will cry quietly. All show respect. Doctors and nurses do their best to make the patient comfortable.'[22]

This is a good time to pray quietly or in silence. In the ritual Pastoral Care of the Sick some beautiful and apt readings are suggested; among these are some verses from the fourteenth chapter of the Gospel of St John. Jesus says:

> Do not let your hearts be troubled.
> Trust in God still, and trust in me.
> There are many rooms in my Father's house;
> if there were not, I should have told you.
> I am going now to prepare a place for you
> and after I have gone and prepared you a place,
> I shall return to take you with me
> so that where I am
> you may be too.
> You know the way to the place where I am going.

Thomas said, 'Lord, we do not know where you are going, so how can we know the way?'
Jesus said:

> I am the Way, the Truth and the Life.
> No one can come to the Father except through me …

> If anyone loves me he will keep my word,
> and my Father will love him,
> and we shall come to him
> and make our home with him.
> Those who do not love me do not keep my words.

Peace I bequeath to you,
my own peace I give you.
Do not let your hearts be troubled or afraid.[23]

I often read through these lines slowly and quietly: they contain much comfort and reassurance. There is no better occasion for a profound understanding of the true significance and value of Scripture. Sometimes the family and I recite the rosary together: they conduct and recite a decade each. We also say the prayer for a good death: 'Jesus, Mary, Joseph, I give you my heart and my soul; Jesus, Mary, Joseph, help me in my final moments; Jesus, Mary, Joseph, let my soul rest in peace with you.' Every morning I conduct a short Eucharistic celebration with readings and prayers in the room of the dying patient. Whoever wishes to receive Communion may do so. At such times public prayer should be kept minimal: it is better to spend more time praying in silence. Praying aloud should only punctuate the silence in order to enrich the vigil at the bedside: it should not serve as a distraction. Each person in the room is allowed the solitude of his or her own thoughts. All are constantly observing the patient, watching and listening for a change in the way the patient lies in bed, or a change in the rhythm of his or her breathing.

It is interesting to observe the various phases each person goes through in reaction to prayer. Some are embarrassed at first, and you can tell that they have not prayed in years. However, in a while, most shed their embarrassment and discomfort. Prayer brings back to God those whom he holds dear, and they express their gratitude and appreciation for all he has done. Just outside the room, people gather in small groups to whisper. Mobile phones ring: friends are calling to ask for news of the patient. Problems pertaining to daily life outside the hospital are forgotten. The outside world seems to have come to a stop. At such times many people have a desire to talk about the fundamentals of life. They often ask questions which are hard to answer.

Doctors and nursing staff have regular meetings with the family to keep them updated about the patient's condition; what medication has been administered; answer any questions.

When death is a long time coming and the agony is protracted for days, the family may indirectly make a request for euthanasia. This has never happened in my presence, but there have been cases, usually when the family of the dying patient were extremely tired or full of anguish at the sufferings of their loved one, that they have asked. A couple of times I have been told that the request had been made by the patient himself. It is terribly painful to watch the gradual dying of the light in a loved one. I must stress, however, that requests of this type have always been motivated by a desire to let the patient be, and not outright requests for euthanasia.

This theme has recently been given a great deal of attention both in the papers and in parliament. The teaching of the Church on the subject is clear: 'Whatever the motives or the means, direct euthanasia consists in the deliberate ending of life of those who are handicapped, sick or close to death. This is morally unacceptable.'[24] Mexican cardinal Javier Lozano Barragán, President of the Pastoral Pontifical Council for Health, has excluded any opportunity for equivocation by the pro-euthanasia camp by stating: 'Euthanasia is the action or the omission of an action for the purpose of securing the death of a person who is terminally ill. In the eyes of the Church this is equivalent to murder plain and simple, and can therefore never be allowable.' The Cardinal does not shut the door on the possibility of making a living will, as long as this does not serve as a Trojan horse for euthanasia.[25]

I hold that the answer to the problem of pain which takes both the feelings of the family and the patient into consideration is palliative treatment. One gets sincere and heartfelt appeals of the type: 'I beg you, allow my father to die; please let him die, he's suffered enough already.' I believe that giving palliative treatment is a humane, morally and legally correct response to such pleas. A person may be helped to die without being killed; it is allowable, from all points of view – the humane, the moral and the medical – to facilitate dying by alleviating pain.

This is what the *Catechism of the Catholic Church* states: 'Even when death is considered imminent, the treatments normally given to a sick person may not legitimately be withheld. The use of analgesics to alleviate the suffering of the dying person, even at the risk of shortening his or her life, may be in moral conformity with the respect of human dignity, as long as these are not administered with the intention of causing death, either as an end in itself or as a means of alleviating suffering, but death is merely foreseen and tolerated as the inevitable outcome. Palliative treatment constitutes an allowable means of being disinterestedly merciful. For this reason it should be encouraged.'[26] The late lamented archbishop of Vienna, Cardinal Franz König, once said: 'At the point of death people should have somebody's hand to hold, but a human hand should never be the cause of death.'[27]

The aim of palliative treatment is to help the dying person by alleviating his pain. It is important to remember that physical pain and the psychological suffering of a person who has only hours left to live are two different forms of pain. Analgesics may obliterate physical pain, but the psychological suffering of the patient continues. It is the doctor's duty to alleviate the physical pain which robs the dying person of his dignity. The anguish caused by the pain cannot, however, be eliminated, because pain does not allow a person to face death with tranquillity. Medical treatment helps, but what is more important at such moments is solidarity, love and the spiritual assistance of those who accompany the dying person.

When a sick person is given treatment which is also an expression of love and humanity accompanied by faith, he or she finds the will to live: as in the case of Mario Melazzini, a forty-eight-year-old father of three, and a consultant at the oncological day hospital of the Salvatore Maugeri Scientific Institute in Pavia. He carries out his duties in this post with great difficulty, since he has been afflicted by Amyotrophic Lateral Sclerosis for the past four years. Melazzini said: 'When I was diagnosed, my first desire was to die. Then I read the Book of Job and understood the importance of asking for and receiving help, and of being able to continue to use one's head.'

When a patient feels that he is a burden to others, and if he does not have proper help, he will often ask for treatment to stop or even to have his life terminated. Such situations are often the true motive behind requests for euthanasia. It is truly a gross lack of love when in some countries, like Holland and Belgium (where euthanasia has been legal since 2002), champions of the welfare state have fallen into the excess of approving euthanasia for the sick, even children, without bothering to ask for the patient's consent.

Doctor Giovanni Battista Guizzetti, geriatric consultant at the Don Orione Centre in Bergamo, has justly stated: 'If one accepts the right to end the life of a patient, one brings about a total change, not only in the doctor-patient relationship, but also in the whole of society.'[28] Doctors and consultants, institutions, political parties and groups must take this change into consideration before campaigning in favour of euthanasia.

Guizzetti cites the Terri Schiavo case. Being in a vegetative state, Terri could not ask to be euthanised. A judge — whether he had the right to do this at all is debatable — granted this right on the insistence of the commercial mass media who took her husband's side against her parents, who absolutely refused to have her euthanised. One must keep in mind that a young American man, who was in a vegetative state for twenty years following an accident, came out of it at the age of forty-two.

The Catholic world, made up of the Church hierarchy, politicians and doctors must create an 'ethical conscience' and must unite to do battle in a coherent and courageous manner. Given that 'human life is untouchable' and 'of non-negotiable value'[29] and that it is already almost too late, they must immediately set about forming public opinion against euthanasia with all means available to them. Some months ago the British Medical Association, representing 130,000 British doctors, voted by a large majority (65 per cent) against the legalisation of assisted suicide and euthanasia.

I should like to conclude this chapter by citing an excerpt from a book entitled *A Way to Die*, written by the parents of a young woman named Jane who was dying in a hospice: 'Sue brought Jane a freshly-cut rose from her garden and placed it on a cushion close to Jane. "I have always wished to wear a rose in my hair," Jane murmured, "but have never had the courage to do so." Making sure that there were no thorns on the stem, Sue delicately placed it behind Jane's ear. From that day on, Jane always wore a rose in her hair. When that first bud bloomed and faded, it was replaced. Whenever the nurses needed to turn Jane over to keep her circulation going or to administer an injection, they would first remove the rose, and replace it when they were finished; Jane's rose and the little bit of velvet were treated gently, as though they were precious. The last rose Jane wore had been picked from the garden outside her window. [...] It was a white rose, just beginning to open. Rosemary (Jane's friend) cut the stem with a pair of surgical scissors. At the hollow centre of the rose formed by the petals was a dew drop. It was an immaculate rose, a perfect rose. Too perfect, Jane would have said: too beautiful to be real.'[30]

NOTES

1   Lk 10:37.
2   M. Petrini, *Caring for the Sick to the End*, Cepsag-Aracne, Rome, 2004.
3   Ibid, p. 231.
4   Pastoral constitution *Gaudium et spes*, 18, 1965.
5   Phil 1:23.
6   Rom 6:4.
7   Cor 1:15, 21.
8   R. M. Veatch, *Death, Dying and the Biological Revolution*, Yale University Press, USA, 1990.
9   E. Bonicelli, *A Return to Life: The Story of a Man's Battle with Leukaemia*, Jaca Books, Milan, 2002, pp. 81–2.
10   Belgian Bishops, 'Accompanying the sick who are close to death', in *Bodies and Souls* 18–182 (1995), 691–701.
11   Pontifical Pastoral Council for Health Workers, *Charter of Health Workers*, Vatican City, 1995, p. 87.
12   M. Petrini, *Treatment Towards the End of Life*, p. 231.
13   Lk 22:39-46.
14   C. Nardi, 'The Agony: Historical Notes on a Human Experience', in *Vivens Homo*, 2 (1996) 293–4.
15   Cor 1:15, 17.
16   Medical-Priesthood Movement, 1st Formation Course, 2003–2004, Scientific Institute of the San Raffaele University Hospital, Milan, pp. 149–50.
17   E. Kübler Ross, *Death and Dying*.
18   Cited in E. Kübler Ross, *Death and Dying*, p. 10.

19   Ibid.
20   P. Vesperien, *Euthanasia*, Pauline Publications, Rome, 1985, pp. 165–6.
21   American Nursing Association, *Code of Ethics*, 1976, 1.6.
22   E. Daly, *Do Not Let Your Hearts Be Troubled*, Veritas Publications, Dublin, 2004.
23   Jn 14:1-6, 23, 27.
24   *Catechism of the Catholic Church*, 2277.
25   *Avvenire (Future)*, 26 September 2006, p. 9.
26   *Catechism of the Catholic Church*, 2279.
27   E. Daly, *Do Not Let Your Hearts Be Troubled*, pp. 50–4.
28   G. B. Guizzetti, *Terri Schiavo and the Hidden Human Being*, Florentine Editing Company, Florence, 2006.
29   National Forum of the Catholic Health Associations.
30   *A Way to Die*, pp. 275–6.

CHAPTER 10

THE ETHICS OF THE INTENSIVE THERAPY UNIT

Whenever I enter an intensive therapy unit (ITU), it is always on tiptoe, even more silently than I go into a church. This section is to a hospital what the tabernacle is to a church, and the patients within it are true images of the crucified Christ. This is where they struggle for their lives, with the dedicated help of medical and paramedical staff. Patients in this unit are in crisis: between 'death and pain' as Elisabeth Kübler Ross states.

I disagree with the view expressed by Umberto Veronesi in the statement: 'The relief of pain collides with, among other things, an archaic Catholic idea of suffering. This may be the reason for the retarded development of Italian medical science in the sphere of pain relief.'[1] I disagree with this because the Church has always shown a special compassion and love towards those who are suffering, which can certainly not be called 'archaic'. The Bible, and above all the New Testament, talks of solidarity, charity, mercy and compassion under the umbrella term *agape*.[2]

One must make a distinction here between pain and *suffering*, as the Italian Episcopal Conference did, and John Paul II in *Salvifici doloris*: they hopefully foresee that pain-relieving interventions may be a means of keeping the introduction of the legalisation of euthanasia at bay. According to ethical principles, the doctor has a duty to treat pain, and not leave the patient to suffer – so much so that the Church is against the preservation of life by extraordinary means.

I remember the case of an adolescent girl who had fallen victim to 'Saturday night fever' at the entrance to a disco. She was in a coma for so long that doctors were in favour of discontinuing life-support. The chaplain could do no more than pray, but even this would have done a great deal to help her mother, who had held vigil in the intensive therapy unit for months. She was inconsolable. The only help I could offer, and for which she was most grateful, was to sit near her in silence, holding a rosary. Almost a year after her ordeal had begun, her faith was rewarded when her daughter was discharged from intensive care. Despite the fact that her daughter had not regained the ability to take care of herself without help, the mother was thrilled.

In such situations, and even in less serious ones, the patient's family is in great need of love, compassion and humanity. The medical staff's professionalism and all the technical equipment that may be available in the hospital are not enough by themselves: it is love that wins the day.

SUFFERING IN INTENSIVE CARE

Ethical questions come up constantly in the intensive therapy unit of a hospital whenever the doctors are faced with the problem of how to deal with a specific case. Medical ethics are not involved solely in the decisions taken on how individual patients should be treated, but also in the professionalism and behaviour of medical staff and in almost every other aspect of clinical care. Ethics involve the management and running of the unit, especially in the consideration of the expense to the hospital, whether public or private. Heads of medical teams and other doctors are often called upon to make ethical decisions in accordance with the code of ethics of medical and paramedical staff, in the absence of which the ITU and medical practice as a whole would be less humane.

In moments of crisis, it is not just the patient's life that is threatened: parents, family and friends also feel threatened. They are made to question their own lives and face the ease with which the human body may be damaged or stop functioning properly. They feel anger and are unable to accept illness and suffering. Not uncommonly, their anger is directed towards God and they will question not only God's motives for the infliction of evil, but his very existence: 'Why has this happened? What has this young person done to deserve such a fate? If there's a God, why isn't he listening to us? This is not a God of love!'

It's useless attempting to answer such questions, which are prompted by an anguish similar to Job's rather than by 'hardened hearts'. In his first encyclical, Benedict XVI wrote: 'Certainly Job may complain to God for the unexplainable and undeserved suffering of this world. These are his anguished words: "If only I knew where to find him, if only I could reach his throne! ... I would discover his answers to my questions and understand what he means. Would he make a show of his power or argue with me? ... This is why I am terrified of him, I think about him and am afraid. God has weakened my heart, the Almighty terrifies me".'[3]

The despairing cries of a mother whose daughter has been rushed to intensive care are not forbidden by God. Like the crucified Christ, she too is calling out, 'My God, my God, why have you abandoned me?'[4]

'Our cries,' Benedict reminds us, 'like those uttered by Christ on the cross, are an extreme way of affirming our profound faith in God's power.' The Pope gives us courage when he says that 'despite being, like all other men, immersed in the complex twists and turns of history, the faithful are kept strong by their certainty that God is our Father and loves us, even though his silence continues to baffle us'.[5]

I have always been convinced – and I have often seen it in their eyes – that all who stand vigil outside the intensive care unit anxious for their loved ones, and who have very little faith in God (some harbouring outright anger towards him), in the end manage to find God, who is both Father and Mother, even if their loved one has died. There was once a chaplain who could not understand why the mother of a young man who was in a coma had said to him, 'Father, please do not come here any more. You may pray if you like'. At times we need silence in order to hear the voice of Christ who speaks with a human and divine compassion that we priests cannot match.

THE PATIENT'S CONSENT
We have listed a number of ethical principles which serve as a guideline for relating with the sick. Many of the principles to be followed in the intensive care unit are legal requirements which vary

from one country to another, even if many states within the European Union have adopted similar norms of behaviour vis-à-vis patients in intensive care. The European Convention on Bioethics, the Declaration of Helsinki and other EU documents confirm many ethical principles common to all member states of the EU.

All agree that the consent of the patient to treatment, which is nowadays required by law, and no longer required only by ethics, cannot be renounced. No medical intervention may be made on an adult patient without the patient's consent, as long as he or she is able to give consent. It is unethical for a hospital receptionist to ask a patient being admitted to sign a consent form without a proper explanation of its details, which can only be given by a doctor. I happened to witness a scene of this kind when an illiterate octogenarian was asked to mark a cross in the space of the required signature on a consent form and the old man refused to comply without a proper explanation of what he was signing.

It is doctors who should inform and explain to patients the details and implications of the consent form. If a patient arriving in ITU is not in a fit state to give his or her consent to treatment, it is up to the doctor to decide, in the best interests of the patient, what are the treatments which will save his life and alleviate pain and suffering.

The patient's consent must be sought before every new treatment is attempted, except in emergency cases where the patient is unable to give such consent and treatment is needed to save the patient's life. In every other case, consent must be volunteered freely and without undue pressure, by the patient in a state of consciousness. The patient is the protagonist and has the right to refuse treatment even if he risks death by so doing; however, according to the law in some countries, the doctor on duty in the ITU may decide on the right treatment of a patient who is not in a fit state to give consent, for the good of that patient.

Sometimes there are very dramatic moments in ITU, as in the case of a fifteen-year-old girl named Sandra who was brought in fighting for life, but whose parents, who were Jehova's Witnesses, refused to sign a consent form for a blood transfusion. This happened around twenty years ago, when there was no clear legislation on such cases.

With Ignazio R. Marino in *Believing and Healing*, I agree that, 'The last word should be his [the doctor's], even at law. Some doctors go along with the present situation, so that they can avoid assuming responsibility for the decisions taken'.[6]

Some jurisdictions, as in Italy, allow a relative (surrogate consenter) to give consent for treatment in the place of an adult who is mentally unfit to do so. In such cases however, the surrogate consenters may not ask for treatment which is not ultimately in the best interests of the patient. Surrogate consenters may be the husband or wife of a patient; adult children; parents; or the closest relative. In the case of child patients, consent may be given by parents, a guardian or another person who has parental responsibility for the child. Minors who request it have the right of consent or refusal of treatment, even though the rights accorded to minors are not the same as those accorded to adults.

PATIENT CONFIDENTIALITY

Medical and paramedical staff are morally and legally obliged to respect the confidentiality and privacy of patients. The medical team may only record information on the condition of patients if this is necessary for treatment. Even when a warrant has been issued for inquiry into the patient, the patient's consent is required before any information may be divulged.

The patient's consent is necessary even for the sharing of information with other medical specialists within the hospital, because the patient has the autonomous right to choose his own medical treatment. In cases of emergency, such as those arising in the ITU, patients are not always conscious and therefore may be unable to give their consent to specific treatments unless there exists a pre-written declaration, or an oral declaration made before witnesses, or a recording made by the patient beforehand on the treatment he desires to be given in case of a future inability to choose.

Living wills

It is no longer rare for patients to make a living will, a practice begun in the USA in the 1960s as a first step made by the pro-euthanasia lobbyists to get euthanasia legalised. As has been stated earlier, Cardinal Javier Lozana Barragán has affirmed that the Church does not intend forbidding living wills. He adds, however, that it is necessary 'to specify whether or not the living will includes the possibility of euthanasia. If so, it is clear that such a document would be unacceptable to the morality of the Church. If, however, the living will is introduced only as a way of refuting the protraction of life by extraordinary measures, then it may be accepted'.[7]

A living will is a document by which the testator leaves anticipatory instructions for doctors outlining the treatment to be carried out in case the said testator should lose the faculties of understanding and volition, or in case a near fatal accident or grave illness should befall the testator, especially if he loses control of his mental faculties. In this will the patient should not be allowed to ask for death, or choose to be allowed to die, for these would be premeditated acts of euthanasia. While respecting the patient's wishes, the doctor must follow professional, legal and ethical codes of conduct and, especially if he is a believer, he must remind the patient's family that life is a gift from God, and therefore to be preserved and not disposed of capriciously.

I remember the case of Francesco, who was in a coma after a terrible road accident not far from the San Raffaele, in which Francesco's friend and his friend's girlfriend were killed. I was called by the doctor in charge of the ITU because Francesco's parents did not agree on what should be done: for months the mother had fought to keep her son alive, but the father wanted him to be allowed to die. 'It's not right that my son should suffer so much,' he said. He was not easily convinced, not being a practising Catholic, that life is a gift from God. Francesco had been a Milan football team supporter and his friends would come and play video recordings of Milan matches for him. After nine months, thanks to his mother's faith and prayers, and much to his father's humiliation, Francesco came out of the coma, to everyone's joy. Some days later I managed to get Ruud Gullit, the famous footballer, to visit him in hospital. (I admired this footballer for the humanity he showed Francesco: his charity, faith and hope clearly came from the heart.)

Doctors in intensive therapy units witness many such 'miracles'.

On being admitted into hospital, patients are often required to sign a living will or a written declaration of which treatments they are willing to undergo should they, subsequent to admission, lose the faculties of understanding and volition. The first legislative documents which anticipated the living will were the Californian Health Service Code and the Natural Death Act, both issued in California in 1976. In these documents it was specifically stated that 'every person could issue directives to prevent the activation or the prolonged use of artificial means of prolonging life in cases which were ultimately terminal'. The law provides that such declarations come into practice thirty days after they have been signed and are valid for three years thereafter. It also allows the doctor leeway for conscientious objection.

A number of Northern European countries, among them Holland, Belgium, Denmark and Germany, have legalised the living will. In these countries, as in the United States, the trend to draw up a living will is on the increase (15 per cent in the USA and around 8–10 per cent in Germany, where this legislation is most recent).

An authoritative document issued by the Guild of Catholic Doctors in the UK states: 'With regard to the drawing up of living wills, a practice originating in the United States in the 1960s as a preliminary step towards the legalisation of euthanasia made by the pro-euthanasia lobby; these may at first glance seem innocuous, or even useful, however the direction this trend seems to be taking shows many signs of soon becoming morally questionable.'[8]

In a living will a patient may declare which treatment he prefers to have or leave clear instructions refusing any treatment at all. Intensive care staff are obliged to respect the patient's wishes, unless the refusal of treatment is a danger to other patients, as in the case where there is danger of contagion with infection or if the patient's wishes are in conflict with the law.

From a Catholic ethical point of view it is very important that the living will should promote and defend the dignity of the human person; that means by being faithful to the Catholic tradition by which it is not obligatory to keep a person alive at any cost by the use of sophisticated equipment – that is, by extraordinary means.

The living will should be an agreement among the patient, his family and the medical and paramedical staff to safeguard quality of life. One must consider its wording very carefully and be aware of the ethical principles it implies and reflects. Some living wills are very vague (as, for example, when they state that it is allowable to withhold food and liquids in a very broad range of situations and conditions); on the other hand there are those which provide for the possibility of euthanasia. A living will formulated by the London Euthanasia Society states: 'Any symptom of discomfort (including that caused by a lack of food or liquid) must be controlled by the use of analgesics or other appropriate pharmaceuticals, even if such therapy should shorten my life.'

The text of the living will formulated by the London Guild of Catholic Doctors, which guarantees to respect ethical principles, is reproduced in the appendix to this present work.

THE LIVING WILL IN ITALY

On 1 March 2006 the Umberto Veronesi Foundation instituted a register of those who would like to make a living will.

In September 2006, in reply to a request for euthanasia made by Piergiorgio Welby, a terminally ill patient, the President of the Republic, Giorgio Napolitano, recommended in a response to parliament that the subject of euthanasia should be reflected upon. This recommendation was manipulated by the media, which misreported or misinterpreted him as having asked for a parliamentary discussion on the subject when in fact what he had really been suggesting was a discussion on the subject by 'the most suitably qualified people'. It would have been more democratic to have held discussions on the subject of the living will with civil society before having an institution like the Senate's Health Commission argue it out. A number of progressively-orientated formulations of the law on the living will, which anticipate the introduction of euthanasia, have been presented in parliament. To these, the Pro-Life Movement has reacted with a sharp and unequivocal 'no to any form of "gentle death"', in the words of its president, Carlo Casini.

As happened with abortion and artificially assisted procreation, a campaign has now been embarked upon which consists of the publication of a spate of films and articles presenting extreme tragic cases, with the aim of turning the tide of public opinion in favour of euthanasia. As Professor Francesco D'Agostino, ex-president of the National Bioethical Commission, has stated: 'as the US experience shows, the application of euthanasia may become a game of macabre bureaucratic banality.'[9]

The National Bioethics Committee (CNB) has expressed its views on the subject by issuing, between 1991 and 2005, five documents about patients who are dying, concerning children and newborns with serious pathological conditions, and adults who are in a vegetative state. In 2003 the committee pronounced itself on the 'Anticipated Declarations of Treatment' which refer to people who express their wishes to their doctors on what treatment they would prefer to be given in case they should lose their faculties of understanding and volition.

The CNB has confirmed that such declarations must not become an excuse for withholding treatment, and that they can only be deemed valid if they respect bioethical criteria. The document should be a public deed drafted in the presence of a notary, for example, and it should contain the date on which it has been drawn up and the signature of the author. It should, moreover, be compiled by a person of legal age who is capable of understanding and volition without any familial, social or environmental pressure. Importantly, it must not bear any predisposition towards euthanasia and must not go against 'good medical practice', the proper code of conduct, the law or ethical behaviour. The committee has proposed that the doctor should study the patient's declaration without, however, the necessity of being bound by it.

The document should reflect the personal will of each patient and be drawn up with the help of a doctor who may, but need not be obliged to, sign it. Printed forms are not considered valid. The discussion of the possible formats this document may take perhaps deserved some more attention from the press, the medical profession and the public.

Since precise regulations on the drawing up of the living will have not yet been passed in Italy, doctors are placed in a very difficult position every time a patient or the family of a patient ask them to suspend treatment. The legislative vacuum on this subject means that doctors and their teams are forced to go out on a limb, legally speaking, and act at their own discretion, knowing that they have no legal protection should things go wrong.

Professor Veronesi has said: 'We should not wait for the next Eluana Englaro [who has been in a coma since 18 January 1992, following a road accident; her father has been involved in a legal wrangle to suspend her life support since 1999] or another Terri Schiavo before we re-open the discussion on artificial life support. Legislators do not realise that the prolonging or shortening of life are no longer values in themselves, but are only valuable in so far as they support the plan each individual has for his/her life. Most patients and an ever-growing number of the healthy population are in favour of the principle of self-determination and equality with the medical profession in terms of their rights and responsibilities. The paternalistic idea that doctors know how best to look after their patients has become as obsolete as have paternalistic attitudes in all social spheres. Faced with medical techniques that are becoming ever more sophisticated, people feel the need to once again take charge of the decisions relating to their own lives and the quality of their lives, every step of the way, including the very last.'[10]

Veronesi has again stated what he has affirmed time and time again: 'I will also fight for euthanasia, but I'll do one fight at a time.' With all due respect, and as his colleague on the Ethical Committee of his European Oncological Institute in Milan, I hope he carries on with his medical vocation of 'treating' and 'curing' patients in their totality as human beings, and forgets about battling and about his proposal of setting up a 'register', so that we may continue to remember Professor Veronesi as the great humane scientist that he is.

This 'register' does not seem either ethical or useful to the community as a whole. During the round table conference of the Science and Rights Committee of the Umberto Veronesi Foundation, organised in Rome on 1 March 2006, Cardinal Ersilio Tonini had this to say about the 'register': 'It seems more like a collection of wills than a desire to extol the virtues of this practice. If I want to make a living will, I can do so through my own notary, and if I want to go back to him and make changes, corrections, or even withdraw it, I can do so. What is the point of creating a "store" of living wills?'[11] From a Catholic ethical point of view, it is necessary to stress the importance of forming the public conscience to properly manage the principle of self-determination, clearly reiterating that the Church does not accept either the extreme prolongation of life or its abbreviation by extraordinary therapeutic measures. It is also only right to point out that this issue does not only concern Catholics.

A few weeks later, I had the honour of inaugurating, together with Cardinal Tonini, the third convention on 'The great new frontiers of oncology', which took place at Villa Bethany in Valderice and was sponsored by the Antonio Campanile Foundation. On this occasion the Cardinal restated his perplexity concerning the 'register' proposed by the Umberto Veronesi Foundation. I too believe that, just like any other will, a living will should be an official document, but it is unethical to publish the names of those who choose to make a living will in a document that is publicly accessible (perhaps even on the internet). I myself have made such a will, and have left it in the care of somebody I trust, who enjoys the high esteem of my family – he is not a medical doctor. Such a will is, to my mind, a tool by which to assert my autonomy regarding God's gift of life to me. Each of us is free to decide whether or not to make such a will.

During a convention held by the Linacre Centre – the Catholic Bioethical Institute – in London, a professor told the story of a patient who had been rushed into intensive care. He was discharged some months later, but before leaving the hospital he visited the professor. After having thanked him, he added: 'I'm glad nobody went through my wallet. If they'd done so, they would have found my living will, and I might have been left to die.'

ATTEMPTS AT EXPLOITATION

On 13 October 2006 the *Corriere della Sera* carried an interview with Fr Luigi Maria Verzè, founder of the San Raffaele Hospital, under the heading 'Don Verzè: I did my utmost to let my friend die', which caused a great stir in the media. Many were happy simply to read the sensational headline and not bother to read on and discover what had really been said in the interview. Others, among whom were the promoters of euthanasia and the living will, called Fr Verzè 'a brave priest' for his 'act of love and Christian charity'. They were trying to manipulate this interview as a means of furthering their cause of introducing a law on anticipated treatment instructions as soon as possible.

Just as the Church itself has done, Fr Verzè has spoken out against the stepping up of extreme therapeutic measures to prolong life beyond reasonable measure, and in no way does he justify euthanasia. He made this amply clear on 16 October following the publication of his interview, in a letter to the editor of the daily *Avvenire*. In this letter he sincerely explained the exact circumstances surrounding an event that had taken place thirty years previously. He wrote: 'In the early 1970s, a dear friend and co-worker of mine suffered an almost complete loss of cardio-pulmonary function. He was attached to a respirator and endured four long months of suffering. He was a convinced Christian who received Holy

Communion daily. Early one morning he called me to his bedside. He was totally alert. I understood what it was he wanted ... I asked the doctors to turn off the artificial life support – to keep him alive as far as they could, without its torment. I was due to leave for Brazil almost immediately, but I knew my friend was still alive after his removal from the respirator. However, after a few days I received news that he had passed away.'

In one of his books Fr Verzè has written: 'It is not permissible to kill because the taking of life is the worst of all evils in the same way as life is the best of all gifts ... euthanasia just seems so irrational, no matter the motive for it. It is a reprehensible act not only from a Christian point of view, but also at scientific and professional levels, demonstrating a cultural vacuum.' He has also stated: 'The brutal nullification of life is not the way to alleviate suffering, nor is the living will registry, which I do not know whether to define as an "evil pact" or a "funereal fridge".' Let us hope that those who have read about the interview in the newspapers or followed the topic on TV now have a clearer idea of what he meant, and have felt some compassion and empathy for this priest who has built a 'hospital for life', the San Raffaele.

'EUTHANAZI'

I once participated in a convention, organised by a lay association, on the subject of euthanasia. Being Catholic, I was accused of wanting to leave sick people in the midst of their suffering, and that of their families, to the bitter end. My belief was judged to be anathema to the dignity and freedom of the individual who has every right to self-determination. This did not surprise me: it is one of the arguments used by promoters of the cause for euthanasia. One pro-euthanasia association in the United States goes by the name of 'Die With Dignity', and the Voluntary Euthanasia Society had even published a booklet containing do-it-yourself instructions on how to commit suicide, which was soon withdrawn from the shelves.

'"Euthanazi": this horrible way of writing the word', wrote Professor Jérôme Lejeune, the man who discovered the genetic anomaly which causes Trisomy 21, 'is not a spelling mistake. It is a historical mistake, for it is a word written in blood.'[12] The word 'euthanasia', derived from the Greek *eu*, meaning 'good' and *thánatos*, meaning 'death', has caused and continues to stir debates and arguments between the promulgators of a secular ethic (although not everybody agrees with it) and those who promote the Christian ethic.

Euthanasia is 'an action aimed primarily at interrupting life' and has been classified as follows:

1. 'Voluntary Euthanasia' – the voluntary murder of those who express a desire to have their lives ended.
2. 'Doctor-assisted suicide' – when a doctor or nurse accedes to the patient's request to help him/her commit suicide.
3. 'Involuntary euthanasia' – the murder of a patient with the collusion of all concerned, apart from that of the patient himself.

In discussing the subject of euthanasia, the media often misuse the terminology and misrepresent the concepts, therefore confusing the public.

THE WORLD-WIDE CODE OF ETHICS

It is the dutiful mission of doctors to do the best for their patients. For the doctors in an ITU this is a daily battle they must fight at their patients' bedsides.

It is ethically wrong to end the life of a patient intentionally, even if the patient has begged one to do so. Anticipated treatment instructions may be followed if they are not too specific or when they stipulate a form of treatment *not* to be carried out. This is also relevant for nurses, especially those working in intensive care and in hospices. The Royal College for Nursing emphasises the difficulty of drafting a living will which is clear and unambiguous.[13] Medical staff are often asked to draw up wills and they should seek the specialised help of a member of the Ethical Committee. The College recommends that nurses should not draft the wording for living wills and should not agree to act as 'proxies/trustees' for patients.

The World Medical Association's Code of Medical Ethics is a very good reference for doctors, especially those working in ITU. This international code of ethics, published in Geneva in 1994, is a modernised Hippocratic Oath which may serve as a guide for solving ethical problems. Below is the list of the norms of practice:

- I solemnly swear to consecrate my life to the service of humanity.
- I will show my teachers the respect and gratitude due to them.
- I will exercise my profession conscientiously and with dignity.
- My patients' health shall be my first consideration.
- I will keep the secrets confided to me even after the death of my patient.
- I will do all in my power to uphold the honour and the noble traditions of the medical profession.
- I will treat my colleagues as brothers and sisters.
- I will not allow age, sickness or disability, creed, ethnic origin, gender, nationality, political ideology, race, sexual orientation or social status to stand between myself and my patient.
- I will hold human life in the greatest respect from its very inception, even if I am endangered by so doing, and I will not use my medical knowledge against the laws of humanity.
- I make these promises solemnly, freely and upon my honour.

BRINGING THE SICK BACK TO HEALTH

One goes to hospital not to die, but to get better, and urgent cases are taken into intensive care to overcome whatever crisis has befallen them. Scientists and doctors carry out research and administer treatment in an attempt to cure the sick. It is not by chance that the San Raffaele Hospital journal, which I edited for almost twenty years, was entitled *Sanare Infirmos*. Christ's command is to 'cure the sick' following on his example.

I've always been fascinated by the Chinese custom of paying doctors for each patient under their care as long as the patient is well. This means that Chinese medicine concentrates on preventing rather than curing illness. This entails regular visits to the doctor's clinic, at times by whole families at once. When a patient becomes ill the doctor's pay for that patient is withheld. We do the exact opposite: we pay our doctors when we are ill.

Medical practice, which consists of prevention and cure through therapy, is expressed in Greek by the one word, *therapéuein*, which means 'to cure, to treat, to serve'. Plato uses the expression *psychén therapéuein*, that is, 'taking care of one's soul'.[14]

This is the vocation and mission of the doctor, founded on a medical anthropology of life and health. As well as the *Ars vivendi,* which may be improved through the prevention of illness, there is also the *Ars moriendi,* and the doctor should not ignore or reject the experience of death. Accompanying a patient to his death is not a defeat. Doctors should not feel helpless in the face of 'sister death', but even if they are non-believers they should consider this aspect of their profession as a sacred art, a noble end, despite the fact that it causes a feeling of impotence.

One cannot discount the efficacy of the prayers which the chaplain and the family (sometimes accompanied by hospital staff), address to God asking for healing for the patient in intensive care. If the doctor is also a 'priest' he cannot underestimate the value of prayer which – as Lord Tennyson wrote – 'works more wonders than the world would believe'. The recovery from illness or trauma is a result of prayer as well as therapy, as may be seen by the Letter of James which reminds us to 'pray for one another and this will cure you'.[15] Communal prayer, the laying on of hands, and a profound faith in Christ the healer and doctor, and in Mary Health-Giver to the Sick, often bring about the gift of healing.

Christ's command was to 'go and proclaim that the Kingdom of Heaven is at hand. Heal the sick … cast out demons'. Christ's healing power flowed through his disciples. In the episode of the epileptic possessed by demons, when the disciples did not succeed in bringing about the epileptic's healing they asked Christ why this should be and he encouraged them to pray more fervently. In the Gospel of St Mark we read that Christ replied to a question similar to the above with the words: 'This is the kind that can only be driven out by prayer.'[16] The same is true of all sickness.

A lady who had been suffering depression for many years decided to put an end to it, despite being surrounded by a loving, caring family. Her attempt at suicide landed her in intensive care in a coma. The doctors tried everything they could but were unsuccessful, until a very spiritual woman, an ex-nun, came and prayed at her bedside, touching her with a miraculous medal of Our Lady. The Lord heard the voice of faith, and after some days the patient came out of her coma.

A friend of mine and his wife had been advised not to have any more children after they had had two, both afflicted with a very rare illness, because the chances of having more sick children were very high. Having great faith in God and in prayer, they went ahead and had two more perfectly healthy children. The father of this friend, an octogenarian former businessman, confided to his son that he had no faith in the after-life. His son replied: 'If there is no after-life better than this one, what would be the point of all the suffering my wife and I have had to endure?'

This is an ethical question which each of us, especially if we happen to be doctors or nurses in intensive care, should ask ourselves when faced with the struggle against death. Health workers do a great deal for patients with their dedication, humanity and generosity. If they added some faith and prayer, they would move mountains.

I have always been inspired by what the 'prophet' Kahlil Gibran (1883–1931), a Lebanese writer and artist who lived in New York, said of prayer: 'Prayer is an entry to God's invisible temple, because it is an "expansion" an "ecstasy" of the individual into "communion" with other human beings.'

NOTES

1   U. Veronesi, *A Caress for Healing*, p. 44.

2   L. Manicardi, *The Face of Suffering*, Qiqajon, Magnano (BI), 2004.

3   Benedict XVI, *Deus Caritas est*, 38.

4   Mt 27:46
5   Benedict XVI, *Deus Caritas est*, 38.
6   I.R. Marino, *Believing and Healing*, p. 76.
7   *Avvenire (Future)*, 26 September 2006, p. 9.
8   Guild of Catholic Doctors, *Advance Directives or Living Wills*, St Paul's, London, 1998.
9   *Avvenire*, 29 September 2006, p. 8.
10 M. Pappagallo, 'Veronesi: Make a Living Will', in *Corriere della Sera*, 1 March 2006, p. 23.
11 L. Liverani, 'Do you have a living will to register?', in *Avvenire*, 2 March 2006.
12 J. Lejeune, *The Message of Life*, Cantagalli, Siena, 2002.
13 Royal College for Nursing, 'Living Wills: Guidance for Nurses', May 1994.
14 E. Borgna and D. Gronemeyer, *Staying Human: High-tech and Heart, Towards a Humane Medical Practice*, Queriniana, Brescia, 2005.
15 Jas 5:16.
16 Mk 9:29.

CHAPTER 11

ETHICS AND THE CARE OF AIDS PATIENTS

My first meeting with an AIDS/HIV patient occurred after I had participated, as a member of the delegation sent over by the Maltese government, in the first health summit meeting held in London and organised by the World Health Organisation (WHO). There were around 148 countries involved in this summit. The Maltese minister of health of the time, the Honourable Louis Galea, had proposed that the concept of 'human and spiritual values' be included in the prevention programme.

On my return to Milan I received a phone call from the distraught mother of a young man, an engineer, who was dying. I immediately visited him in hospital. (There I was surprised to find a young American patient in the neighbouring bed telling the beads on his rosary. He said to me: 'The rosary is my medicine.' From then on, I saw my young American friend through to the end, constantly reciting the rosary with him.)

The death of their only son was an immense sorrow to the parents. Since their son had been an active believer, it came as a great shock to the mother that, as she tearfully recounted, the parish priest would not allow the funeral of somebody who had died of AIDS in his church, as the parents had wished.

I was astounded by the parish priest's attitude, and even more so when I learned the reason for his refusal: 'Holding the funeral of an AIDS victim in the church endanger[ed] the health of [his] parishioners,' he said to me.

It was only my presence and the fear of the story getting into all the newspapers that swayed the parish priest's conviction enough to allow me to officiate at the funeral in the end. He himself never appeared at the ceremony, however. Fortunately, there are many religious, both men and women, all over the world who generously do their utmost to help AIDS patients, and I believe that this parish priest was an exception to the rule.

AIDS is not a punishment sent by God, nor is it a shame or a plague. It is a global challenge which should inspire society to solidarity with its victims and motivate rich countries to compassion and generosity towards countries with fewer human and material resources than they themselves have.

DRUGS AND THE FAMILY

I came into direct contact with the 'mystery' of AIDS/HIV when I was director of CISF. Before organising the international conference on 'Drugs and the Family', I felt the necessity of visiting a number of rehabilitation centres in order to familiarise myself with the problems involved in such cases. It was during this 'pilgrimage' of mine to various communities scattered throughout Italy and beyond, that I learnt at first hand of the rehabilitation work being carried out by the Community of San Patrignano. I also came to know the pioneers in the battle against drugs. Among these: Vincenzo Muccioli, Fr Mario Picchi, Fr Luigi Ciotti, Fr Gino Rigoldi, Fr Antonio Mazzi, Franco Marchesini, the sisters of Cascina Verde in Segrate, and the indefatigable brothers Fr Pierino and Fr Eligio Gelmini of the Friars Minor. These were my teachers.

Along with the above-mentioned workers in the field, there were experts from twenty-five countries (Australia, Canada, Finland, India, Iran, Ireland, the United States, Sri Lanka, Zaïre and most European countries) participating at that conference, which at the time was termed an 'historic event'. Also present were the Honourable Oscar Luigi Scalfaro, then Italian minister for home affairs; Dom Helder Câmara, Archbishop of Olinda and Recife in Brasil, known as 'the brother of the poor'; and Cardinal Carlo Maria Martini. There was also a televised video message from Nancy Reagan, wife of the US president of the time.

I had invited the charismatic leaders of the principal rehabilitation communities to two preparatory meetings in order that they might exchange ideas and experiences. Surprisingly, it transpired that they had never met before this occasion, as there was no national network of communication coordinating the communities: each cultivated his/her own vineyard in isolation.

In 1985, as a follow-up to the conference, I decided, in collaboration with psychiatrist Massimo Clerici and psychologist Valentina de Rosa, to publish a document entitled 'A White Paper on Drug Prevention'. This collaborative document was aimed at filling in the lacunae in the field of drug prevention: often a less attractive undertaking than the setting-up of therapeutic or welfare frameworks.

It was fashionable, at the time, to talk of drug prevention, but the methodologies, the models and the relative know-how were non-existent. In fact this document is still valid today, many years after its publication.

Following this work, the United Nations organised a forum on 'Drug Abuse and Trafficking' in Vienna in 1987. I presented our book at this forum and reaffirmed that it is in spiritual values that 'young people often find the answer to their inadequacies; their spiritual emptiness; their lack of direction in life and their hunger for love'.

THE CENTRE FOR THE CARE OF AIDS PATIENTS

It was the will of Providence that I should carry all this accumulated baggage of experience to the San Raffaele Hospital Scientific Institute, which was at that time involved in research on diabetes: for which reason, as Fr Luigi Verzè stated at the opening of the first convention on AIDS in this building, some people were not in favour of starting new research in the field of AIDS. On the occasion of the international convention on 'AIDS: Ethics, Justice and Health Policy', also held at the San Raffaele in October 1991 and attended by fifty North American and European experts, the same Fr Verzè stated: 'Our Institute could not remain insensitive to the challenge of AIDS. The plight of AIDS sufferers had to be addressed even by ourselves, in our habitual way: by putting together the scientific knowledge at our disposal; the expertise gained over so many years of service in the care of the sick; the constant holistic formation of our healthcare personnel. Humanitarian and Christian motives have led us to bear witness to this plight in many parts of the world.'[1]

These events cumulatively proved to be the seed which eventually blossomed in the construction and inauguration, on 12 October 1991, of the San Luigi Centre for Infectious Diseases and the Treatment of AIDS, one of the first of such centres in Italy.

On the occasion of one of the days dedicated to Life, Fr Verzè had remarked to me, just before Holy Mass: 'St Carlo Borromeo sold the silver candlesticks belonging to the Milan Duomo (Cathedral) to be able to succour plague victims when the city was struck by plague. What is the San Raffaele doing for AIDS sufferers?' I do not know where the money financing this project eventually came from, but at the hospital entrance appears a prominent sign which reads: 'All is possible for he who believes.' The other Raffaellian credo is 'faith works'. And in fact, the whole of the San Raffaele complex, comprising branches both in Italy and overseas, is the fruit of a sound, live faith which is totally prepared for sacrifice.

The San Luigi Centre today boasts forty beds and is considered the 'golden tabernacle' of what has been termed 'The Temple', dedicated to medicine and the alleviation of suffering. It is such work which inspires the sick to find hope of relief through science and medicine, and gives hope to the families of the sick, who would otherwise be prey to desperation: only faith can fill the void of separation following the illness and death of a loved one.

Through their company and care, the doctors, priests, researchers, nursing staff and all other workers at the San Luigi Centre transmit such hope to the patients.

COMPASSION FOR AIDS SUFFERERS
In the book *Seven Last Words*, by Fr Timothy Radcliffe,[2] who used to be Dominican General, an icon by artist Frances Meigh is

reproduced. The icon is entitled 'Compassion for AIDS Sufferers' and it greatly moved me; it had been commissioned by the English Dominican Province in the 1980s, when people were beginning to take notice of the new illness. Fr Radcliffe described the suffering of those struck with AIDS thusly: 'They suffer because they are excluded and isolated.'

In those days, the health prospects of industrialised nations seemed rosy. The most common causes of death were cardiovascular disease and cancer, and these were progressively being brought under control by new therapies and surgical innovations. Indeed, in this day and age there are scientific cures for such illnesses: Professor Umberto Veronesi, reported in the daily *La Repubblica* on 11 June 2006, states: 'Cancer deaths all over Europe have for the first time lessened by about 10 per cent in the past five years, and this reversal has no doubt been brought about by preventive medicine. For Italy, this statistic represents over fifteen thousand fewer deaths per year.'

However, back in the 1980s, the widespread complacency in developed countries with regards to health was suddenly shattered by the death, on 30 March 1984, of Gaetan Dugas, the first officially recognised AIDS victim: 'patient zero'. Since then, despite all progress made in research and treatment, and despite the fact that it is not easily contagious, AIDS has spread rapidly through the world and is especially rampant on the African and Asian continents.

The English Dominicans, and we also, have reflected on the dramatic reality of AIDS. Fr Radcliffe had this to say: 'A young man, dying in hospital, had to drag himself out of bed to reach his food as nobody dared carry it into his room. It seemed to us that welcoming AIDS sufferers would be a witness of our faithfulness to the Gospel. One small initiative was to commission the artist Frances Meigh to execute this icon depicting Compassion for AIDS Sufferers.' Inspired by Michelangelo's 'Pietà' to be found in St Peter's Basilica in Rome, but differing from it in that while Michelangelo's work shows a dead Christ in the arms of his seated Mother, Meigh's painting shows 'the young AIDS victim alive, lying in the arms of the resurrected Christ. In the background, one can see the cross on which

Christ had been crucified, its cross-beam like wide-open arms welcoming all those who are emarginated; because in this icon, the body of Christ has AIDS.'[3]

One here becomes aware of the humanity of Christ the Healer who watches over AIDS sufferers and invites them to live through this illness, together with their loved ones, offering up their sufferings to him. Even those who are afflicted with AIDS will one day win the battle with death and rise again. Christ's invitation, to those who already suffer from AIDS, and to all its potential victims, upholds and respects their full human dignity. When medicine seeks the support of faith, it becomes more effective.

AIDS AND THE PATIENT

The topic chosen for the 'Ethics and AIDS' conference was 'AIDS: A Time for Healing, a Time for Action'. This conference took place 5–7 September 1989 in Adelaide, Australia, and was very well attended. Many of those present were young HIV/AIDS sufferers. In my opening speech I added to the theme slogan the phrase 'AIDS: a time for ethics'. As a matter of fact, the Australian government's programme had not given much thought to ethics. Acquired Immuno-deficiency Syndrome (AIDS) and Human Immunodeficiency Virus (HIV) do not merely pose medical problems, but also, and perhaps more importantly, pose ethical problems because they involve the whole person.

Because AIDS is transmittable, it has raised a multiplicity of personal and social problems beyond the purely medical. AIDS poses a combination of medical, legal, social, economical and, last but not least, ethical problems.

AIDS often places the rights of the individual in conflict with the rights of society, for even human rights have their limits. Hence the United Nations' Convention on Human Rights may be deemed a proper blueprint, ethically speaking, on which to base the confrontation of the AIDS problem. For example, Article 8 (of the Convention on Human Rights) protects the rights to intimacy, to independence and to the freedom of the individual to choose his own destiny, while Article 5 reminds us that 'no individual may be deprived of his/her freedom ... except in the case of somebody carrying a contagious disease, who must be isolated'.

The European Council was quick to intervene when measures which went against the Convention on Human Rights were adopted in order to combat the spread of AIDS; especially when certain emergency measures ran the risk of causing discrimination against sections of European populations.

AIDS and HIV raise problems which require a many-pronged interdisciplinary approach for their solution. We need to bring to them a broad vision integrating medical, legal, economic, political and ethical problems. It is only by adopting this holistic approach that the human person is considered in totality. Such a combination of disciplines may stimulate a synergistic approach to the problem.

If we are considering the human person in its totality, we cannot exclude the ethical angle. We cannot only identify with some aspects of the AIDS phenomenon to the exclusion of others: this would be unethical.

At times, the ethical angle is avoided for fear of entering into conflict with what some may consider controversial moral values about which it is difficult to reach a consensus in a pluralistic society. Nevertheless, it is possible to focus on a pluralistic totality of values without conflict.

For this reason, ethics should not be viewed as some kind of moral judgement. Illnesses cannot be judged: ethics are not a rule-of-thumb by which one may judge what 'is and is not done', nor should they be a restriction on human freedom. Ethics reduced to moral norms do not remain ethics.

When we speak of ethics, in some way we are talking about ourselves, about our own values, our own convictions and our own way of life. Far from being mere theory, ethics are very practical because they give flesh to the totality of the human person as body and soul.

The ethical point of view issues from the marriage of our inner being and our environment. As John Paul II said, we are called to be 'the ethical conscience of society'.

In my opinion, based on my experiences with AIDS sufferers, there are four guiding principles which should be part of the ethos of all hospitals:

1. *Respect for the Autonomy of the Individual*

   Autonomy implies the absence of coercion and the respect of the individual's right to be consulted in any decisions regarding his/her treatment. This also included the right to freedom of choice, to give informed consent to treatment, and to privacy.

2. *The Collective Well-Being of the Community*

   Morality requires not only that we treat individuals autonomously and that we refrain from harming them, but also that we safeguard the health of the entire community. This may at times involve restrictions upon individual freedom in order to prevent the suffering of others. Here the principles of charity and the duty to avoid harm come into play. These are hard to separate: they imply that one individual should not inflict harm or offence on another, but on the contrary should remove the causes of harm or that which is offensive, and be the promoter of the well-being of another. The Hippocratic oath 'Primum non nocere', 'First do no harm' must be applied both on an individual and on a collective level.

3. *The Principles of Solidarity and Social Justice*

   Consequently to the points listed above, one must foster mutual help and justice in order to achieve the good of each member of society. The word 'justice' refers also to social justice whereby both the rewards and the duties are equally distributed. This involves cooperation within a society in a spirit of human solidarity on all aspects: moral, legal, medical and cultural.

4. *The Fostering of Human Values*

   This involves the careful assessment of what is right or wrong, and the rights and duties of the individual. Such is the *ethic of virtue* and it does not refer to any single rule on what should or should not be done. 'It is, rather, a habit, or disposition, or trait of character, which a person may have or may aspire to have.'[4] It is a trait of character that inclines the person who possesses it to act according to moral principles, norms or ideals.

To *human values* as emerged from the WHO recommendations in London, I have no hesitation to add *spiritual values* (which are not necessarily solely religious values). The human conscience often transcends human values. As Beauchamp and Childress state, 'ethical theory alone does not make for morality. It can only throw light on morality by analysing and assessing moral justifications. Ethics require thought, while morality must be lived'.[5]

The Christian virtue of love and charity, which is also evident in human solidarity, is the basis of our proposed ethic. The patient afflicted with AIDS 'is my brother or sister', to whom I owe my love and compassion. Love becomes tangible when we are faced with situations of suffering, injustice and poverty. It is an extraordinary fact that no medical aspect of HIV has escaped ethical examination. All this is part and parcel of 'good clinical practice' because it recognises the importance of patient confidentiality; the duty to require patient consent before taking any therapeutic measures or conducting any medical examination; the importance of counselling HIV-positive patients on their duties towards sexual partners; the medical and psychological help to women patients on the subjects of procreation and the prevention of transmission of the disease to others; insurance issues; issues at the place of work etc. Nowadays these and other similar matters pose questions to ethicists, doctors and even governments, in relation to their health policies.

Other ethical implications concern behaviour, which is doubtlessly the hardest part of the problem because it entails a total change of lifestyle regarding interpersonal relations and sexual behaviour in order to prevent transmission of the disease. At this juncture we are faced with the dynamics between individual and liberal ethical values and the pursuance of the common good for the health of the community, beginning with one's own partner. We need to instil new confidence in, and to strengthen the resolve of, those who are at risk.

FEAR AND AIDS

Who, among those at risk of contracting HIV or AIDS, is not afraid? Many young people live in fear beneath the sword of Damocles, but they often do not have the will power or the ability to extricate themselves from their precarious situation. Despite having been infected they continue to lead promiscuous lifestyles and although they live in fear, they continue to mix freely with others to whom they might transmit their infection.

Health workers are not immune to the fear of contagion with AIDS, and adequate precautions must be taken by them. However, apart from the danger of contagion, working in health centres specialising in the treatment of AIDS patients may also lead to 'burn-out' as I recall happened to some young nurses who generously offered to care for AIDS patients in the first years of the spread of this disease, when AIDS-related deaths were more frequent than they are today.

In 2004 it was reported to me that AIDS patients at the San Francisco General Hospital were increasingly refusing intensive and respiratory treatment. Other hospitals deny AIDS patients such treatments on the basis of the argument that 'a patient who is considered dead does not need treatment'. A survey conducted among 258 New York doctors towards the end of the 1990s had shown that 25 per cent of them considered it perfectly ethical to refuse treatment to AIDS patients, causing the American Association of Medicine to intervene with the statement that 'a doctor may not ethically refuse to treat a patient whose condition he or she is competent of treating simply because that patient has AIDS or is HIV-positive'.[6]

Fear undoubtedly causes negative repercussions on patients, and in some cases it may lead to suicide or to the isolation of those patients who refuse to leave their homes and face people. At times, those who are not ill with AIDS behave very unethically, inhumanly and unchristianly towards AIDS sufferers for fear of contracting their disease. In the early years of the initial spread of AIDS, surveys showed that the majority of people were in favour of quarantining suspected AIDS carriers and of obligatory screening.

Some, like the evangelist William F. Buckley, campaigned in favour of tatooing anybody with AIDS, in the same way as the Nazis had done with concentration camp inmates. Others, like the extremist Islamic theologian Abdallah Al-Machad (1989) in Cairo, actually proposed the execution of AIDS sufferers. And there were those who believed that the treatment and care of AIDS patients placed too great a financial strain on governments.

After her battle with cancer, the well-known writer Susan Sontag wrote a monograph entitled *AIDS and its Metaphors*, containing profound reflections on the metaphors and attitudes by which this illness is judged and distorted, and about the way society, led by the mass media, describes AIDS through punitive apocalyptic imagery. To give an example, it is enough to quote a few of the expressions used in the labelling of AIDS, some of which are that it is a 'curse against humanity', 'God's punishment', 'the plague of the century'. And there have been those who have gone further, comparing AIDS with leprosy, and the world with Sodom and Gomorrah.

Aristotle wrote: 'Metaphor consists of giving something the name of another thing.' Metaphor has, in the past and to this day, been a potent rhetorical device. Susan Sontag reminds us that there is no occasion for surprise here, since throughout human and medical history, the plague has always been used as a metaphor for the worst calamities, for evil and punishment.[7]

To some, as Sontag states, AIDS has become synonymous with 'evil', 'sin', 'perversion' and 'shame'. Hence the illness becomes a thing that must be hidden, because the patient fears being judged as promiscuous; as having indulged in aberrant sexual behaviour; as a drug addict or a homosexual. At times there have been Christians, and even men of the Church, who have shown very little evidence of charity by favouring the 'psychological terrorism' fomented by the mass media.

AIDS is therefore perceived as a terrifying 'enemy', and some past governments, such as that of President Reagan, declared 'war on AIDS' and 'war on drugs'. The illness is often viewed as some kind of 'invasion of alien organisms'.[8] I am in total agreement with Sontag's statement that 'the military metaphor describes AIDS in an exasperated fashion, mobilises the population against AIDS victims and greatly contributes to their emarginisation and stigmatisation'.[9] The war metaphor only serves to feed the fears of the public.

The best actions to be taken for the good of the whole community are prevention, education and the promotion of human and spiritual values. An attitude of compassion and love forms the basis of our solidarity with AIDS sufferers. A beautiful example of this is contained in a pastoral letter by Cardinal Joseph Bernardin, Archbishop of Chicago. In his letter, Cardinal Bernardin had stated: 'When we help those afflicted with AIDS, we should do so in a Christ-like spirit of love and compassion. Rather than judging them, we should attempt to convert and heal them. Our touch should be one that heals.'

Another beautiful exhortation came from his friend, Cardinal Basil Hume, Archbishop of Westminster, who, with great humility and serenity, stated: 'Nothing is gained by recrimination against any one sector of the population whom we may hold responsible [for the spread of AIDS]. We should, rather, show a tangible and unconditional compassion to AIDS victims. Nor would it be a right or moral course of action to take the law into our own hands in the pursuit of what we deem to be justice. We must do something a great deal more radical and constructive than attempting to break what we perceive to be the bad habits of other people.'

The Anglican Archbishop of York, the Right Reverend Dr John Habgood, made a very pertinent observation: 'If we associate AIDS too closely with moral weakness, we are being unjust with those who contract the disease through no fault of their own: for example, young brides who might contract AIDS because their husbands do not know they are infected with it; babies who contract the disease from their mothers; haemophiliacs. If the disease is made to carry a moral stigma, then we are simply adding to the burden of suffering which those afflicted with it have to bear.'

One may also remember the example given by the holy Mother Teresa of Calcutta, who, in the early years of AIDS, on seeing young people dying on the streets of New York, said, as she had done in Calcutta about her 'Home for the Dying': 'We cannot simply watch. We must roll up our sleeves and help.' Her motto was 'A heart to love and hands to help'. I have seen evidence of her works both in Calcutta and New York, where every Thursday the Archbishop of the time, Cardinal Joseph O'Connor (whose beatification cause is in process) would go to bless the sick and help with their nursing. He gave his help in whatever was needed, and by his love won many souls.

ATTENDING TO AIDS SUFFERERS

The preceding paragraphs have been important in illustrating the establishment and fostering of the 'culture of life' which is indispensable if we are to attend to the needs (both physical and spiritual) of AIDS/HIV sufferers. It is necessary that we form an 'ethical conscience' through scientific knowledge and awareness of the problems posed by AIDS. Those who dedicate themselves to the care of AIDS patients need support and psychological formation. To be able to give of their best, they must also be professionals of great human sensitivity.

Caring for an AIDS victim involves accompanying him or her through all the phases of the illness – most importantly in that last phase, when AIDS is full-blown – according to the ethical principles of *solidarity, compassion and professionalism*. It is essential that the rights of the sick, as well as those of their carers, be respected.

As we have seen, the first gesture of acceptance towards AIDS sufferers is empathy: it is vital to listen to what the sick have to say in order to better understand how they live their illness. Experience has taught me that the first treatment such people need is the stimulus to tell their own story.

On one occasion, Cardinal Martini intended coming to the San Luigi Centre to visit a priest who had contracted a contagious illness. The Cardinal meant to stay for about fifteen minutes; however, I suggested that he should come on a day when he had more time at his disposal in order to be able to visit for a few hours in case the AIDS patients felt the need to open their hearts to him. He took up my suggestion and we set a date for a time when he could make a longer visit. Martini came to the centre, and with great humility and serenity listened to the stories of many of the young AIDS patients who found a 'father' in him.

Among the rights of HIV-positive patients is the right to medical treatment equalling that of any other citizen, whether for complications arising from their condition or for other clinical problems totally unrelated to it. This may seem obvious; however, where no 'ad hoc' arrangements exist, AIDS and HIV patients often do not receive the treatment they need. At the San Luigi Centre, I have often met young patients who come from central and southern Italy, where there is a lack of specialised clinics and organisation to deal with their specific treatment. The same happens in other hospitals, for example the excellent clinic for infective illnesses at the Sacco Hospital in Milan, which is headed by Professor Mauro Moroni, one of the leading Italian specialists in the sector.

The spiritual care of these patients is one of the most demanding, delicate and important, because priests, chaplains and volunteers bear witness to Christ-as-Healer. The priest or chaplain shares in the suffering experienced by the young patients, but he emerges purified from this experience, spiritually strengthened and enriched. Helping these young people face death without fear is truly a great gift from God working through the priestly charism. When these patients arrive at the hospital in the final stages of their illness, they have often touched rock-bottom but they meet Christ through the priest and their other carers. Then the illness becomes a *kairos*, an occasion for conversion, for, as Aristotle taught, every tragedy is resolved in a catharsis.

AIDS AND THE USE OF CONDOMS

As a priest who has lived among married couples and among the sick for over fifty years, I cannot discuss the problem of AIDS prevention without touching on the extremely ethically controversial question of the use of condoms as a preventative measure for the spread of AIDS.

I shall introduce this topic starting with the AIDS pandemic in Third World countries in order to make some ethical observations about behaviour and the possible strategies for fighting the spread of AIDS. According to the 2005 WHO estimates, there are about forty-two million carriers of the AIDS virus world-wide. Add to these the three million who have already died of AIDS and the five million new cases registered each year, to give a complete picture.

I remember the words of Professor Roland Bayer of Columbia University during the 'Discussion on AIDS' held at the San Raffaele: 'None of us are safe as long as there is even a single person who has AIDS in the world. The only thing to be done is to say no to a society which behaves as though nothing were happening.' It is for this reason that we must ask ourselves how we can ethically confront this illness in order to stop its progression, especially in the poorest and most depressed countries where AIDS has reached pandemic proportions.

AIDS affects both adults and children. In an article published in *The Lancet* in 2006 appear the results of a study conducted jointly by the World Health Organisation and the universities of Harvard and Queensland (Brisbane, Australia) on the number of AIDS and HIV victims world-wide. Each year, around 3.6 million people die; of these 20 per cent are children below the age of five. Ninety-nine per cent of infantile deaths occur in Third World countries (more than 40 per cent of these in sub-Saharan Africa). These are shocking statistics considering the fact that the deaths are caused by AIDS and malaria.

The child victims of AIDS often contract the disease from their mothers, while still in the womb. The above-quoted study reports more statistics which provide food for thought: in 2004 alone, in Zimbabwe, thirty-six thousand of the total fifteen million deaths were of children; in Botswana, 40 per cent of the population is HIV-positive, as are 38 per cent of the pregnant women. Kenya holds the sad record of having the highest incidence of HIV, with approximately 1.3 million people who are HIV-positive.

The situation appears even more shocking when we remember that only 1.3 million of Africa's AIDS-afflicted populations, totalling 6.5 million, have access to any form of medical treatment. The greater scandal is the fact that governments lack the financial means of treating these patients: the cost of medicines is too high, despite the aid of international agencies like the United Nations Organisation and the World Health Organisation, and Catholic organisations like Caritas.

Pope Benedict XVI himself stated on World AIDS Day 2006 that the numbers of people suffering from AIDS have reached truly alarming proportions. Offering medical and financial help is not enough in the face of such a drastic situation: it is ethically necessary to formulate strategies of prevention. The Church is not indifferent to the situation, even if it has nothing new to say about the use of condoms in preventing the diffusion of AIDS.

Some burning questions posed by journalist Ignazio Marino to Cardinal Carlo Maria Martini in an interview,[10] were: 'How acceptable is the refusal to promote the use of condoms as a preventative measure of the spreading of AIDS?'; 'Is it the duty of governments to decide on this question?'; 'As regards Catholic doctrine, should the acceptance of the use of condoms as a preventative measure, contributing to the saving of so many human lives not be regarded a lesser evil?'

Cardinal Martini replied clearly to these questions: 'The statistics you quote are tragic. In the western world it is very difficult to understand the suffering of some nations. Having visited them myself, I have witnessed this suffering, borne for the most part in silence and with great dignity. We must do all in our power to fight AIDS. Certainly, in some situations the use of condoms may be seen as a lesser evil. There are, for example, situations such as that of married couples where one partner is afflicted with AIDS. The affected partner is *obliged to protect the other* and the healthy partner must protect him or herself. But the true question is whether it should be the religious authorities who promote such a mode of defence, thereby implying that other methods, including abstinence, be classified as second options, and risking the encouragement of irresponsible behaviour. Therefore, accepting the principle of the lesser evil as being applicable in all cases covered by an ethical doctrine is one thing, but publicly condoning the use of condoms is quite another. I believe that prudence, and the consideration of the diverse local situations may allow each person to effectively fight AIDS without encouraging irresponsible behaviour.' Cardinal Martini is not alone in expressing such a view. One of the countries worst hit by AIDS is Burundi, where 70 per cent of the 7,600,000 inhabitants are Catholic. According to UNAIDS, about 6 per cent of the population were afflicted with AIDS in 2003, and the number must have grown since then.

In March 2006 the country's episcopal conference concluded that, before being able to marry, engaged couples must demonstrate certification of having undergone an HIV test. Respecting personal privacy, the bishops do not demand that the results of the test be shown, but they insist that there be medical attestation showing that the test has taken place, and they exhort engaged couples to be truthful with one another.[11]

It must also be said that the bishops do not deny anybody, even the sick, the right to be married; above all else, their aim is to educate couples on prevention. This is the stance held by the Church in many African countries, and some bishops in South Africa had at first been very open-minded about the use of condoms.

It is worth citing the case of Bishop Gilles Côté of Daru-Kinnga (Papua New Guinea) who, according to the London weekly *The Tablet*, is working hard to fight the AIDS epidemic on that poor Pacific island. He has declared himself to be in favour of the government's distribution of condoms 'since pre-marital sexual relations, and those between various partners are commonplace'. According to this prelate, 'if an infected person has unprotected sex, he or she will infect other people. It is therefore a moral responsibility to insist that other people's lives be safeguarded'.[12]

One of the most authoritative declarations on the subject in Europe was that made by Cardinal Godfried Danneels, Archbishop of Malines-Brussels and member of the Military Order of Brussels, who considers the use of condoms a 'lesser evil' in the fight against the mortal illness of AIDS. The Cardinal asserts that if a sick man has sexual relations with his wife, she may oblige him to wear a condom, otherwise 'he would be committing the grave sin of murder'. He adds: 'If condoms are used for the sake of protecting human lives, this is no longer a sexual problem. Without the condom, a person is at risk.'[13]

The two most authoritative documents on this subject are those by Cardinal Alfonso López, President of the Pontifical Council for the Family, dated 1 December 2003; and by Cardinal Javier Lozano Barragán, President of the Pontifical Council for Health, dated 1 December 2005, on the occasion of World AIDS Day.

Both documents show the position of the Church on the use of condoms in the prevention of AIDS. In his document entitled 'Family Values and So-called Safe Sex', Cardinal López asserts: 'My position has always been decidedly against so-called "free love" and promiscuity, which is nowadays encouraged by certain permissive political measures and sections of the media. This is why I reminded listeners [he is here referring to an interview granted to the BBC on 12 October 2003] that the Church teaches a moral position which is valid for all: believers and non-believers.' He adds: 'Protective sheaths do not give enough protection against AIDS/HIV and STDs [sexually transmitted diseases]; I was also referring to the permeability of condoms as demonstrated by scientific experiments. It must be pointed out that the AIDS virus is 450 times smaller than the spermatozoon, and that there are various other risks involved in the use of the protective sheath due to its structure and because it may easily be mishandled or wrongly placed.'[14]

To sum up, the salient points contained in the above-mentioned document are the following:

I.   'The Catholic Church has repeatedly criticised the promotion of condoms as a fool-proof method of AIDS prevention. Various episcopal conferences all over the world have expressed anxiety over this issue.' Cardinal López cites the bishops of South Africa, Botswana and Swaziland who categorically state that the promotion and distribution of condoms as a means of preventing the diffusion of AIDS/HIV is 'both immoral and mistaken'. On this point he also cites the episcopal conferences of Spain, the Philippines and the United States as well as the authoritative moralist Cardinal Dionigi Tettamanzi, present Archbishop of Milan, and his 'voluminous book entitled *New Christian Bioethics* published in 2000'.[15]

2.   The stance adopted in non-ecclesiastical quarters is also very interesting. López cites the book by Dr Helen Singer-Kaplan, *The Real Truth about Women and AIDS*, where the author affirms that 'counting on condoms is flirting with death'.[16] He also cites the *Dutch Medical Journal*, which has expressed grave 'preoccupation stemming from the fact that the AIDS virus is about twenty-five times smaller than the head of the spermatozoon, 450 times smaller than its length and sixty times smaller than the syphilis bacillum'.[17]

Yet another authoritative source cited by Cardinal López is the World Health Organisation, which states that 'the regular and correct use' of the condom reduces the risk of HIV infection by 90 per cent. However, 'there is a risk of condoms tearing or slipping ...'[18]

The International Planned Parenthood Federation (IPPF) has given an even lower percentage of protection, stating that 'the use of a condom reduces the risk by 70 per cent compared with the total protection afforded by sexual abstinence. This estimate is consistent with the results obtained in the majority of epidemiological studies'.[19]

Cardinal López further cites a wide range of scientific records which show the relative lack of success of the condom both in the prevention of pregnancy and of sexually transmitted diseases.

Cardinal Barragán's document had been intended as a message on the occasion of World AIDS Day. In this short document the Pontifical Council on Health for the ecclesiastical Ministry of Health unites with UNAIDS which 'each year organises a world-wide campaign for the fight against AIDS'. The Cardinal makes mention of the fact that '26.7 per cent of centres for the treatment of AIDS patients in the world are Catholic' and names the Good Samaritan Foundation set up in 2004 by Pope John Paul II 'in order to provide economic help, from donations received, to the most needy patients in all parts of the world, and in particular to AIDS/HIV victims'.[20]

The Cardinal does not broach the subject of condoms, but focuses on prevention and the promotion of 'the stability of the family and the education of children in the correct understanding of sexual activity', exhorting governments to 'promote the health and well-being of all their citizens with special attention to AIDS victims on the basis of the principles of responsibility, solidarity, justice and equality'. He addresses the pharmaceutical industry, scientists, health workers and the mass media, exhorting them to 'furnish the public with unbiased, clear, correct and truthful information on the AIDS/HIV phenomenon and on methods of prevention, without any attempt at exploitation'.[21]

Because these two pontifical councils fall under the ministry of the Holy See, one may clearly understand the official position of the Church from the above *excursus*.

MUSIC AND LUKE'S DEATH

I recall a person whom I shall here name Luke, from whose face all traces of youth had been wiped out by twenty-odd years of alcoholism, heroin use and promiscuity. When called by a friend to his room, I had thought he was an elderly man. I went there because I felt that Christ had done so much for me, it was now my turn to give to others his Word of Life, his Mercy and, above all, his Love. Luke hugged me and cried like a babe in arms. He did not need to speak, for in that hug I understood his great suffering and need for love.

He told me his story. I listened to the very end. Despite his having stayed away from the sacraments after his Confirmation, I knew he was a religious soul. He kept asking for Christ's love and forgiveness and imploring the mediation of the Caravaggio Madonna. He cried and was very afraid in the face of death, for the doctors had told him the truth about his condition. He professed his faith in God but confessed that there had been times when he had felt abandoned by all: his parents, his wife (by whom he had a daughter) and even God.

While I was with him, however, he admitted that he no longer felt alone because he felt the presence of God. He asked to be allowed to see his dear ones, especially his eight-year-old daughter. Human love caused the miracle which brought God's love to Luke.

Truly, God is love. It is marvellous to see how the power of God's love enters, touches and caresses suffering humanity.

Luke loved Mozart and Vivaldi as well as modern music. Day and night he would listen to the song 'I Believe in Miracles' by the Jackson Sisters, a song I was familiar with as I had heard it during a Mass for young people in Cape Town, South Africa, some years previously.

In my years among the sick, I have encountered a predilection for the biblical psalms in patients, who find them very meaningful and often ask for a copy to keep at their bedside. There have been times when I have written out phrases from the Psalms in brightly-coloured ink for patients to keep in front of them. Some examples of these are:

- The Lord is my Shepherd, I shall not want (Psalm 23)
- I call to the Lord and he answers me (Psalm 120)
- Those who trust in the Lord … are unshakeable, standing for ever (Psalm 125)
- I love the Lord for he listens to my plea (Psalm 116)
- Oh God, come and save me (Psalm 69).

In the space of a few weeks, Luke's condition worsened a great deal. He was aware of this, and would say, 'Christ is coming to take me'.

He had become resigned and serene in the knowledge, brought about by his reconciliation with God, that a new and better life awaited him. He had succeeded in becoming detached from all worldly things and from every person, apart from his little daughter. He died to the sound of 'I Believe in Miracles' and clutching St Benedict's Cross in one hand. The words of Georges Bernanos 'grace is all' in his *Diary of a Country Curate* ring profoundly true. It is a hard thing to say, but for these young people sickness is a powerful occasion for the revelation of God's love.

GIVING HOPE TO THE SICK

Being among AIDS sufferers pushes us constantly to take up the challenges posed by this pandemic. Doctors, nurses and other health workers, chaplains, the families of the sick: their parents, partners and friends, are especially called upon to follow the example of the Good Samaritan, and care for these people, who are often left alone by the wayside. When we come across these patients we must, like the Good Samaritan, 'be compassionate', and prepared to 'bandage their wounds, pouring oil and wine on them'.[22]

It is not up to us to 'moralise' and judge, but up to the merciful Lord who is both Father and Mother. To us is assigned the role of accepting, supporting and helping these people. We must not forget that the first need of these patients is to be heard with empathy. Over and above that is the importance of giving them hope to live, for left alone, such people often do not have the will or the desire to stay alive. Their hope is in Christ, the God who makes himself a patient like themselves, and who promises eternal life.

Ethics generate hope: hope in mankind; in science and medicine; in life. Even as far back as the second century, Cicero recalls, in his letter to Atticus the maxim which still holds true today: '*dum anima est, spes est*, where there is life there's hope.'[23] This refers to sincere, not false, hope.

We may find it hard to pronounce the word 'hope' at a time when AIDS appears to be a global pandemic, but this word is not meant as a metaphor, nor is it merely a consolatory utterance. Scientific research has made great strides, and nowadays, even AIDS sufferers may be hopeful of a longer, fuller and more normal way of life than heretofore, thanks to new forms of therapy.

This hope, which had already been raised during the fifth World Conference on AIDS organised in Montreal, Canada, in June 1989, and attended by 10,000 doctors, scientists and diverse health workers, grows ever stronger.

It was at this conference that I met Brenda Mason, a housewife in her thirties who had been accidentally infected with AIDS through a transfusion with contaminated blood while she was in labour with her second child. When we met in Montreal she said: 'I believe that I am about to become a member of the first generation to witness the transformation of AIDS into a chronic and curable illness.' Even if we do not yet have at our disposal the means of defeating AIDS once and for all, scientific research is on the right track. This hope is not that of a single individual, but is collective, and we pray that it may soon become global.

I conclude this chapter with a quotation from Pope Benedict XVI on this theme: 'Closely following the example of Christ, the Church has always considered the care of the sick an integral part of its mission. For this reason I applaud the many initiatives undertaken, most especially by Christian communities, for the eradication of this illness, and I feel close to all those who are afflicted with AIDS and their families, and invoke upon them the help and comfort of the Lord.'

NOTES

1   *AIDS: Ethics, Justice and Health Policy*, San Raffaele Hospital Scientific Institute, ed. Paolo Cattorini, Edizione Paoline, Cinisello Balsamo, Milan, 1993, pp. 21–2.
2   T. Radcliffe, *Seven Last Words*, San Paolo, Cinisello Balsamo, Milan, 2004, pp. 72–3.
3   Ibid., p. 72.
4   T.L. Beauchamp, J.F. Childress, *Principles of Biomedical Ethics*, Le lettere, Firenze, 1999, p. 261.
5   Ibid., p. 276.
6   American Association of Medicine, 1987, p. 7.
7   S. Sontag, *AIDS and its Metaphors*, Farrar, Strauss & Giroux, New York, 1988, p. 45.
8   Ibid., p. 9.
9   Ibid., p. 94.
10 'A Discussion on life' in *L'Espresso*, April 2006.

11 *The Tablet*, London, 1 April 2006.

12 Ibid., 8 April 2006, p. 33.

13 Ibid., 18 March 2006.

14 A. López Trujillo, *Family Values and So-called Safe Sex*, 1 December 2003, no. 1.

15 Ibid., nos. 2–4.

16 Dr Helen Singer-Kaplan is the founder of the Human Sexuality Programme of the New York Weill Cornell Medical Centre, Cornell University.

17 A. López Trujillo, op. cit., no. 6.

18 *The Guardian*, Special Report, 13 October 2003.

19 A. López Trujillo, op. cit., no. 6. See also W. Cates, 'How Much Do Condoms Protect Against Sexually Transmitted Diseases?', in IPPF *Medical Bulletin* 31/1 (February 1997), pp. 2–3.

20 Address by Cardinal Javier Lozano Barragán on the occasion of World AIDS Day, 1 December 2005, nos. 1–7.

21 Ibid., no. 8.

22 Lk 10:33-34.

23 G. Ravasi, *Return to the Virtues*, Mondadori, Milan, 2005, p. 92.

A CHRISTIAN ADVANCE DECLARATION FOR THE MANAGEMENT OF SERIOUS ILLNESS

I CONSIDER LIFE IN THIS WORLD A GIFT AND A BLESSING FROM GOD, BUT NOT THE SUPREME AND ABSOLUTE VALUE. I KNOW THAT DEATH IS INEVITABLE AND THAT IT PUTS AN END TO EARTHLY LIFE, BUT I HOPE AND PRAY THAT IT OPENS MY WAY TO FULLNESS OF LIFE WITH GOD.

THE FOLLOWING PARAGRAPHS ARE INTENDED TO DIRECT THOSE WHO MUST MAKE DECISIONS FOR ME SHOULD I BECOME UNABLE TO DO SO. I WISH TO RECEIVE MEDICAL TREATMENT APPROPRIATE TO MY CONDITION AND WHICH OFFERS A REASONABLE HOPE OF BENEFIT. IN NO CIRCUMSTANCES WOULD I WISH BASIC CARE, INCLUDING (IF APPROPRIATE TO MY CONDITION) THE ASSISTED ADMINISTRATION OF FOOD AND FLUIDS, TO BE WITHDRAWN WITH THE AIM OF ENDING MY LIFE. I ASK THAT WHEN FACED WITH THE IRREVERSIBLE APPROACH OF DEATH, I BE PROVIDED WITH ORDINARY NURSING AND MEDICAL CARE, INCLUDING PAIN RELIEF, APPROPRIATE TO MY CONDITION.

NOTHING SHOULD BE DONE WHICH WILL DIRECTLY AND INTENTIONALLY CAUSE MY DEATH, NOR SHOULD ANYTHING BE OMITTED WHEN SUCH OMISSION WOULD DIRECTLY AND INTENTIONALLY CAUSE MY DEATH. I FORBID EUTHANASIA (AN ACTION OR OMISSION WHICH OF ITSELF OR BY INTENT CAUSES DEATH), WHETHER BY COMMISSION OR OMISSION.

I ASK THAT IF I AM IN DANGER OF DEATH, I BE TOLD OF THIS SO THAT I MAY PREPARE MYSELF FOR IT. IF I AM UNABLE TO MAKE DECISIONS FOR MYSELF, I DIRECT THAT MY SPIRITUAL NEEDS BE TAKEN CARE OF AND THAT, IN PARTICULAR, THE ATTENDANCE OF A ROMAN CATHOLIC PRIEST/MINISTER* BE IMMEDIATELY REQUESTED, WHO SHOULD BE INFORMED OF THE GRAVITY OF MY CONDITION.

DATE AND SIGN THE FORM HERE IN THE PRESENCE OF TWO
WITNESSES:

DATE: _____

SIGNATURE: _____

IN THE PRESENCE OF: _____

(THE WITNESS MUST SEE YOU SIGN ABOVE AND THEN SIGN HERE,
AND PRINT HIS/HER NAME AND ADDRESS)

SIGNATURE OF WITNESS: _____

NAME: _____

ADDRESS: _____

OCCUPATION: _____

(THE WITNESS MUST SEE YOU SIGN ABOVE AND THEN SIGN HERE,
AND PRINT HIS/HER NAME AND ADDRESS)

SIGNATURE OF WITNESS: _____

NAME: _____

ADDRESS: _____

OCCUPATION: _____

THIS DOCUMENT REMAINS EFFECTIVE UNTIL I MAKE IT CLEAR IN
WRITING, OR AT LEAST IN THE PRESENCE OF NOT FEWER THAN
THREE WITNESSES, THAT MY WISHES HAVE CHANGED.

*I WOULD PREFER: (NAME AND ADDRESS OF PRIEST OR MINISTER IF
AVAILABLE)

PATRON SAINTS OF VARIOUS ILLNESSES

In the history of the Church the saints are 'lights' which God has placed on our path to show us his infinite holiness. The Church, as Mystical Body of Christ, lives the communion between the pilgrim people of God and the Heavenly Church which lives the beatitude.

The authentic cult of the saints does not so much consist of the multiplicity of exterior acts but rather of the intensity of our active love which is translated into a commitment to Christian life. The ultimate aim of the veneration of the saints is the glorification of God and the sanctification of man. In the lives of the saints the Lord offers us an example; by their intercession he offers us help; in the communion of grace, a bond of brotherly love.

It is therefore very right that we should love these friends and co-heirs of Christ who are also our brothers and distinguished benefactors, and thank God for them. We turn to them in supplicant prayer and depend on their prayers and powerful aid in beseeching God's grace through his Son Jesus Christ, our Lord and only Saviour and Redeemer. In fact every true attestation of love we make to the saints, by its very nature reaches and ends with Christ, who is the 'king of all saints', and through him reaches God, whose wonder is shown to us and glorified in his saints. The list has been provided by the Pontifical Council for Health of the Holy See, whom we thank.

Abdominal Colic
St Agapitus
St Charles Borromeo
St Erasmus

Acute delirium
St Dionysius
St Peter the Apostle
St Ulric

Alcoholism
St John of God
St Martin of Tours
St Matthew the Apostle

Angina
St Swithbert

Animal illnesses
St Beuno
St Dwyn
St Nicholas of Tolentino

Appendicitis
St Erasmus

At the point of Death
St Abel
St Barbara
St Benedict
St Catherine of Alexandria
St James the Younger
St John of God
St Joseph
St Margaret of Antioch
St Michael the Archangel
St Nicholas of Tolentino
St Sebastian

Barrenness, Sterility, Difficulty of Conception
St Agatha
St Anne
St Anthony of Padua
St Casilda of Toledo
St Egidio
St Henry II
St Felicity
St Fiacre
St Philomena
St Francis of Paula
St Margaret of Antioch
St Rita of Cascia
St Theobald Roggeri

Blindness
St Cataldo
St Cosma
St Damian
St Dunstan
St Leger
St Lawrence the Illuminator
St Lucy
St Lutgarda
St Odile
St Paraskeva
St Raphael the Archangel
St Thomas the Apostle

Bone fractures
St Drogo
St Stanislaw Kostka

Breast illnesses
St Agatha

Childbirth
St Erasmus
St Gerard Maiella
St Leonard of Noblac
St Lutgarda
St Margaret of Antioch
The Blessed Virgin Mary
St Raymond Nonato

Childhood illnesses
St Aldegonda
St Beuno
St Clement I
St Farailde
St Ubaldo Baldassini
St Hugh of Lincoln

Convulsions
St John the Baptist
St Willibrord

Convulsive Fits in children
St John the Baptist
St Guy of Anderlecht
St Scholastica

Cough
St Blaise
St Quentin
St Walpurga

Cramps
St Cadoc of Llancarvan
St Maurice
St Pancras

Deafness
St Cadoc of Llancarvan

St Drogo
St Francis de Sales
St Meriadoc
St Ouen

Desire for pregnancy
St Andrew the Apostle

Desperate Cases and Lost Causes
St Jude Thaddeus
St Gregory Thaumaturge
St Philomena
St Rita of Cascia

Disabilities
Blessed Alpaïs of Cudot
St Angela Merici
St Egidio
St Henry II
St Gerard of Aurillac
St Germain Cousin
St Lutgarda
Blessed Margherita di Città di Castello
St Seraphina
St Servazio
St Servolo the Paralytic

Drunkenness
St Bibiana

Dumbness
St Drogo

Dysentery
St Lucy
St Polycarp of Smyrna

Ear Problems
St Cornelius
St Polycarp of Smyrna

Eczema and other skin conditions
St Anthony the Abbot
St George
St Marculfus
St Peregrine Laziosi
St Rocco

Epidemics
St Godeberta
Our Lady of Zapopan
St Rocco

Epilepsy
St Alban of Mainz
St Anthony the Abbot
St Baldassar
St Bibiana
St Cataldo
St Cornelius
St Christopher
St Dymphna
St Genesio
St Gerard of Lunelio
St John the Baptist
St John Chrisostom
St Guy of Anderlecht
St Egidio
St Valentine
St Vitus
St Willibrord

Equine illnesses
St Eligio

Erysipelas
St Anthony the Abbot
St Benedict
Blessed Ida of Nivelles

Fainting fits
St Urban of Langres
St Ursus of Ravenna
St Valentine

Fever
St Adelard
St Amalberga
Blessed Andrew Abellon
St Antonino of Florence
St Benedict
St Castor
St Claude
St Cornelius
St Domenic of Sora
St Domitian of Huy
The Four Crowned Saints
St Genoveffa
St Gereberno
St Gertrude of Nivelles
St Giudoco
St Mary of Oignies
St Nicostratus
St Petronilla
St Peter the Apostle
St Raymond Nonato
St Sempronius
St Severus of Avranches
St Sigismund
St Theobald Roggeri
St Hugh of Cluny
St Ulric
St Winnoc

Fistulae
St Fiacre

Gall Stones
St Benedict
St Drogo
St Florian of Strasburg
St Liberius

General illness
Blessed Alphonse of India
Blessed Alpaïs of Cudot
St Angela Merici
St Angela Truszkowska
St Arthelais
St Bathilde
St Bernardette of Lourdes
St Camille de Lellis
St Catherine of Siena
St Catherine Dei Ricci
St Drogo
St Edel Quinn
Blessed Elisabeth of the Trinity
St Philomena
Blessed Gerard of Villamagna
St Germain Cousin
St John of God
St Julie Billiart
St Julia of Nicomedia
St Juliana Falconieri
St Gorgonia
Blessed Isabelle of France
Blessed Jacinta Marto
St Lidwina of Schiedam
St Luis IX
St Louise of Marillac
St Mary Anne of Paredes
Blessed Maria Bagnesi

Blessed Maria Gabriella Sagheddu
St Mary Magdalen of Pazzi
St Maria Mazzarello
Blessed Marie Rose Durocher
St Michael the Archangel
Our Lady of Lourdes
St Paola Frassinetti
St Peregrine Laziosi
St Raphael the Archangel
St Rafka Al-Rayes
St Catherine Dei Ricci
St Syncletica
St Theresa of Avila
St Theresa of the Andes
St Thérèse of Lisieux
St Theresa Valsè Pantellini
St Hugh of Lincoln

Goitre
St Blaise

Gout
St Andrew the Apostle
St Killian
St Colman
St Gereberne
St Gregory the Great
St Maurice
St Mauro
St Totnano

Haemorrhage
St Lucy of Syracuse

Haemorrhoids
St Fiacre

Headache

St Acacio
St Anastasius the Persian
St Bibiana
St Dionigi Aeropagita
St Gerard of Lunelio
St Gereone
St William Firmato
St Pancras
St Stephen the Martyr
St Theresa of Avila

Health

The Christ Child of Prague

Heart diseases

St John of God

Hernia

St Drogo
St Florian of Strasburg
St Osmund

Hernias

St Alban of Mainz
St Castaldo
St Conrad of Piacenza
St Cosmas
St Damian
St Drogo
St Gomer

Herpes Zoster (Shingles)

St Anthony the Abbot

Hoarseness

St Bernardino of Siena
St Mauro

Ictus

St Andrew Avellino
St Wolfgang

Infant death

St Alphonsa Hawthorne
Blessed Angela of Foligno
St Cyriac of Iconium
St Clothilda
St Conception Cabrera de Annida
Blessed Dorothy of Montau
St Edwidge
St Elisabeth Ann Seton
St Elisabeth of Hungary
St Felicity
St Frances Romana
St Judith
St Isidore the Farmer
St Joaquina Vedruna de Mas
St Leopold the Pius
St Lucius
St Luis IX
St Margaret of Scotland
St Marguerite of Youville
St Mathilda
St Melanie the Younger
St Michelina of Pisaro
St Nonna
St Perpetua
St Stephen of Hungary

Inflammations

St Benedict

Intestinal ailments in children
St Erasmus

Invalidity
St Rocco

Jaundice
St Odilon

Kidney troubles
St Benedict
St Drogo
St Margaret of Antioch
St Ursus of Ravenna

Knee troubles
St Rocco

Labour Pains
St Ann
St Erasmus
St John of Brindlington
St Margaret of Antioch
St Margherita Fontana
St Mary of Oignies

Leg troubles
St Servazio

Leprosy
St Egidio
St George
St Lazarus
St Vincent de Paule

Livestock epidemics
St Beuno

Longevity
St Peter the Apostle

Lumbago
St Lawrence

Mental illnesses and depression
St Benedict Joseph Labre
St Bibiana
St Christina
St Dymphna
St Drogo
St Egidio
Blessed Eustace of Padua
St Fillan (Foelan)
St Job
St Margaret of Cortona
Blessed Maria Fortunata Viti
St Michelina
St Osmund
St Raffaella
St Roman of Condat
St Verano

Migraine
St Gereone
St Severus
St Ubaldo Baldassini

Nervous Tics
St Bartholomew the Apostle
St Cornelius

Neurological illnesses
St Bartholomew the Apostle
St Dymphna

Obsession
St Quirinius

Ocular illnesses
St Cornelius
St Polycarp of Smyrna

Pain
St Madrone

Paralysis
St Cataldo
St Osmund
St Wolfgang

Pestilence
St Anthony the Abbot
St Cosma
St Christopher
St Damian
St Aloysius Gonzaga
St Rocco

Plague
St Hadrian of Nicomedia
St Cataldo
St Colman
St Cuthbert
St Edmund of East Anglia
St Erhard of Ratisbon
St Francis of Paula
St Francis Xavier
St George
St Genoveffa
St Gregory the Great
St Macarius of Antioch
St Rocco
St Sebastian
St Valentine
St Walpurga

Pregnancy
St Ann
St Anthony of Padua
St Elisabeth
St Gerard Maiella
St Joseph
St Margaret of Antioch
St Raymond Nonato
St Ulric

Rabies and Hydrophobia
St Dominic of Silo
St Guy of Anderlecht
St Otto of Bamburg
St Sithney
St Hubert of Liège
St Walpurga

Rheumatism and Arthritis
St Colman
St Killian
St James the Elder
St Servazio
St Totnano

Scrofula
St Balbina
St Mark the Evangelist
St Marculfus

Sexually Transmitted Diseases
St Fiacre

Smallpox
St Matthew

Somnambulism
St Dymphna

Spasms
St John the Baptist

Spontaneous Abortion
St Catherine of Siena
St Catherine of Sweden
St Eulalia
St Monica
St Urbanus of Langres

Stammering
Blessed Notker the Stammerer

Stomach ailments
St Brizio
St Carlo Borromeo
St Erasmus
St Timothy
St Wolfgang

Sudden death
St Aldegonda
St Andrew Avellino
St Barbara
St Christopher

Sydenham's chorea (St Vitus's dance)
St Vitus

Syphilis
St Fiacre
St George

The inability to produce breast milk
St Margaret of Antioch

Throat ailments
St Andrew the Apostle
St Blaise

St Ethelreda
St Godelieve
St Ignatius of Antioch
St Lucy
St Swithbert

Toothache
St Apollonia
St Kenan
St Christopher
St Elisabeth of Hungary
Blessed Ida of Nivelles
St Médard
St Osmund

Tuberculosis
St Pantaleone
St Thérèse of Lisieux

Tumours
St Aldegonda
St Egidio
Blessed Giacomo Salomone
St Peregrine Laziosi

Whooping cough
St Blaise
St Winnoc

Wounds
St Aldegonda
St Marciana
St Rita of Cascia

Patron Saints of medical
professionals

Anaesthetists
St René Goupil

Blood Banks
St Gianuario

Clinical Records Officers
St Raymond of Peñafort

Dentists
St Apollonia
St Foillan

Dieticians
St Martha

Doctors
St Cosma
St Damian
St Luke the Apostle
St Pantaleone
St Raphael the Archangel

Healers
St Brigid of Ireland

Health-Service Workers
St John Régis

Hospital Administrators
St Basil the Great
St Francis Xavier Cabrini

Hospital Public Relations Officers
St Paul the Apostle

Hospital Technical Staff
St Albert the Great

Hospital Workers
St Camille of Lellis
St John of God
St Jude Thaddeus
St Vincent de Paul

Hospitals
St Camille of Lellis
St Elisabeth of Hungary
St Erhard of Ratisbon
St John of God
St Jude Thaddeus
St Vincent de Paul

Knights Hospitallers
St John the Baptist
St John the Almsgiver

Nurses
St Agatha
St Alexius
St Camille de Lellis
St Catherine of Alexandria
St Catherine of Siena
St John of God
St Margaret of Antioch
St Raphael the Archangel

Nursing Aides
St Catherine of Siena
St Elisabeth of Hungary

Pharmacists
St Cosma
St Damian
St Gemma Galgani
St James the Elder
St James the Younger
St Nicholas of Mira
St Raphael the Archangel

Radiologists and Radiotherapists
St Michael the Archangel

Surgeons
St Cosma
St Damian
St Follian
St Luke the Apostle
St Rocco

Veterinary Surgeons
St Blaise
St Eligio
St James the Elder

BIBLIOGRAPHY

Ariano, G., *Pain for Growth*, Armando Publishing, Rome, 2005.

_____*Person-Centred Therapy*, Giuffrè, Milan, 1990.

Beauchamp, T.L. and Childress, J.F., *Principles of Biomedical Ethics*, Le Lettere, Florence, 1999.

Bianchi, E. and Manicardi, L., *Living With the Sick*, Qiqajon, Magnano (BI), 2000.

Bianchi, E., *I Was a Stranger and You Welcomed Me*, Rizzoli, Milan, 2006.

Bonicelli, E., *A Return to Life: The Story of a Man's Battle with Leukaemia*, Jaca Books, Milan, 2002.

Borgna, E. and Gronemeyer, D., *Staying Human: High-tech and Heart, Towards a Humane Medical Practice*, Queriniana, Brescia, 2005.

Cappel, C., *Let Me Run Away*, Messaggero Publishing, Padova, 2005.

Cattorini, P. (ed.), *AIDS: Ethics, Justice and Health Policy*, Paoline Publications, Cinisello Balsamo (MI), 1993.

Comolli, G.M., *Brother Man and Sister Truth: A Simple Path Through the Problems of Bioethics*, Gabrielli Publishing Imprint, Verona, 2006.

Cornaglia Ferraris, P., *White Coats and Pyjamas: The Doctors' Part in the Disastrous Italian Health Service*, Laterza, Bari, 2001.

_____*Pyjamas and White Coats: Changes in the Italian Health Service*, Laterza, Bari, 2000.

Daly, E., *Do Not Let Your Hearts Be Troubled*, Veritas Publications, Dublin, 2004.

Demmer, K., *Fundamentals of Theological Ethics*, Cittadella Publishing, Assisi, 2004.

Fornero, G., *Catholic Bioethics and Secular Bioethics*, Mondadori, Milan, 2005.

Gandolfo, E., *Gregory the Great, Servant of the Servants of God*, Vatican Library Publishing, Vatican City, 1988.

Guerriero, E. (ed.), *Testimonials of the Italian Catholic Church: From the 1900s to the Present*, San Paolo, Cinisello Balsamo (MI), 2006.

Guild of Catholic Doctors, *Advance Directives or Living Wills*, St Paul's, London, 1998.

Guizzetti, G.B., *Terri Schiavo and the Hidden Human Being*, Florentine Publishing Society, Florence, 2006.

Kirkwood, Neville A., *Pastoral Care in Hospitals*, Morehouse Publishing, London, 1995.

Kübler Ross, E., *Death and Dying*, Cittadella Publishing, Assisi, 1979.

Lejeune, J., *The Message of Life*, Cantagalli, Siena, 2002.

Leone, S., *The Theological Perspective in Bioethics*, Sicilian Bioethical Institute, Palermo, 2002.

Lewis, J.M., *Being a Therapist: How to Teach it and How to Learn it*, Martinelli, Florence, 1981.

Liverani, L., 'Do You Have a Living Will to Register?' in *Avvenire (Future)*, 2 March 2006.

Malherbe, J.F., *Towards a Medical Ethic*, Paoline Publications, Cinisello Balsamo (MI), 1989.

Manicardi, L., *The Face of Suffering*, Qiqajon, Magnano (BI), 2004.

Marino, I.R., *Faith and Healing*, Giulio Einaudi Publishing, Torino, 2005.

_____'A Discussion on Life', Interview with Cardinal Carlo Maria Martini in *L'Espresso (The Express)*, 16 April 2006.

Martini, C.M., *An Exploration of the Vocabulary of Ethics*, Piemme, Casale Monferrato (AL), 1993.

McKenna, B. and Libersat, H., *Miracles Do Happen*, Veritas Publications, Dublin, 1987.

Messori, V., *A Stake on Death*, Sei, Torino, 1982.

Moriconi, B., *Job: The Weight of Suffering, The Strength of Faith*, Camilliane Publications, Torino, 2001.

Nagle, V., *On the Frontier of the Human: A Priest Among the Sick*, Rubettino Publishing, Soveria Mannelli (CZ), 2004.

Nardi, C., 'The Agony: Historical Notes on a Human Experience', in *Vivens Homo* 2, 1996.

Pappagallo, M., 'Veronesi: Make a Living Will', in *Corriere della Sera*, 1 March 2006.

Pastoral Pontifical Council for Workers in the Field of Health, Health Workers' Charter, Vatican City, 1995.

Pellegrino, E., *For the Good of the Patient: Tradition and Innovation in Medical Ethics*, Paoline Publications, Cinisello Balsamo (MI), 1992.

Pellegrino, E. and Thomasma, D., *Medicine as a Vocation*, Dehoniane Publications, Rome, 1994.

Petrini, M., *Treatment at the End of Life*, Cepsag-Aracne, Rome, 2004.

Radcliffe, T., *Seven Last Words*, San Paolo, Cinisello Balsamo (MI), 2004.

Ratzinger, J., *Servants of Your Joy*, Ancora, Milan, 2002.

Ravasi, G., *Qohelet and the Seven Sicknesses of Being*, Qiqajon, Magnano (BI), 2005.

_____*A Return to the Virtues*, Mondadori, Milan, 2005.

Reich, W.T., *Encyclopaedia of Bioethics*, The Free Press, New York, 1978.

Rogers, C.R. and Kinget, G.M., *Psychotherapy and Human Relations*, Boringhieri, Turin, 1970.

Rogers, C.R., *Client-Centred Therapy*, Martinelli, Florence, 1970.

Salvino L., *The Theological Perspective in Bioethics*, Sicilian Bioethical Institute, Palermo, 2002.

Salvino, L. and Privitera S., *A New Dictionary of Bioethics*, Città Nuova, Rome, 2004.

San Raffaele Scientific Institute, First Formation Course, 'Medicine and Priesthood', San Raffaele, Milan, 2003–2004.

Sgreccia, E., *A Manual for Doctors and Biologists*, Vita e Pensiero, Milan, 1986.

Sontag, S., *AIDS and its Metaphors*, Farrar, Strauss & Giroux, New York, 1988.

_____*Humanising Sickness and Death*, Vita e Pensiero, Milan, 1986.

Spinsanti, S., *Humanising Sickness and Death*, Paoline Publications, Cinisello Balsamo (MI), 1980.

Tettamanzi, D., *Man as God's Image: Fundamental Issues of Christian Morality*, Piemme, Casale Monferrato (AL), 1992.

_____*Bioethics: A New Challenge for Mankind*, Piemme, Casale Monferrato (AL), 1987.

_____*Euthanasia: The Illusion of the Good Death*, Piemme, Casale Monferrato (AL), 1985.

Tramarin, A., *The Sick Hospital: Economics and Medicine in Hospital Management*, Marsilio Publishing, Venice, 2003.

Tumino, S., *Christ Heals Your Heart*, Rinnovamento nello Spirito Santo Publications, Rome, 2002.

Veatch, R.M., *Death, Dying and the Biological Revolution*, Yale University Press, USA, 1990.

Vella, C.G., *Caring: The Family and the Patient, an Interdisciplinary Approach*, ed. Vittorio Alessandro Ferrari, Ferrari Publishing, Bergamo, 2003.

_____*The Family Planning Clinic and the Family Counsellor*, AVE Publications, Rome, 1978.

Veronesi, U., *The Right to Die: The Freedom of the Secular Person in the Face of Suffering*, Mondadori, Milan, 2005.

_____*A Caress for Healing: The New Medicine, A Balance of Science and Conscience*, Sperling & Kupfer, Milan, 2004.

A Note on the Author

Charles G. Vella was born in Malta in 1928. Between 1948 and 1955 he studied philosophy and theology at the Pontifical Gregorian University and the Venerable English College. He was ordained in Rome, for the archdiocese of Malta, on 8 December 1954. In 1956, after a time spent working with the 'Family Institute' in Chicago, he founded the Cana Movement, offering marriage preparation to engaged couples and counselling to married couples. In 1962 he trained in communications with the BBC in London and took charge of the running of Maltese Radio and Television stations, a post he held until 1975. He was United Nations consultant for the International Year of the Aged and of Children.

In 1972 he began a collaboration with CEI (Italian Bishops' Conference) for the setting up of family counselling centres, establishing himself as 'a pioneer of pastoral family care' (Archbishop Cosmo Francesco Ruppi). In 1974 he was nominated director of CISF (International Centre for Family Studies) instituted by the San Paolo Periodicals Group in Milan; he founded the monthly magazine *Family Today* and was one of the founding members of the 'Italian Confederation of Christian Family Planning Clinics'. Since then he has directed around thirty-five two-year formation courses for staff working in family planning clinics in various parts of Italy.

In 1986 he was asked to take over responsibility for the Public Relations Office of the Milan San Raffaele Hospital's Scientific Institute, and to edit the house organ of the hospital, *Sanare Infirmos*. In that same year the Maltese government nominated him as its representative to the European Council in Strasbourg on the Ethical Committee and the Social Policy Committee. He served as president of the latter for four years. Since 1988 he has been a member of the Milan European Oncological Institute's Ethical Committee (IEO).

In 2000 he was nominated spiritual director of the International Confederation of Christian Family Movements (ICCFM). On the occasion of the World Day of the Family, 16 May 2006, he was invited to give an address to the European Parliament in Strasbourg on the subject of the problems besetting the family today.

He has written many books, among which are: *Marriage Counselling; The Family Planning Clinic and the Family Planning Consultant; Love and the Couple; From Bioethics to Ethical Committees;* and two volumes on Marriage Preparation Discussion Group Meetings. The anthology entitled *Caring: The Family and the Patient, an Interdisciplinary Approach* (ed. V.A. Ferrari) is a collection of works by the author.

In 1994 he was made Monsignor by Pope John Paul II. He was also made Honorary Canon of the Archdiocese of Lublin, Poland in 1996. He has been honoured with the Order of Merit of Malta (1993); is a Knight of the Italian Republic (2004); a Knight of the Order of Hospitallers of St John of Jerusalem (2005); an Honorary Canon of the Diocese of Prato (2008); and a Prelate of the Knights of the Holy Sepulchre (2008).